T0065511

The Art of Leading Scripture Recitations

To speak the Word clearly and naturally with an understanding that animates the passage.

Thomas L. Griffin

WESTBOW
PRESS®
A DIVISION OF THOMAS NELSON
& ZONDERVAN

Archway Publishing books may be ordered through booksellers or by contacting:

Archway Publishing
1663 Liberty Drive
Bloomington, IN 47403
www.archwaypublishing.com
844-669-3957

ISBN: 978-1-6642-2936-5 (sc)
ISBN: 978-1-6642-2938-9 (hc)
ISBN: 978-1-6642-2937-2 (e)

Library of Congress Control Number: 2021906896

Print information available on the last page.

Archway Publishing rev. date: 5/18/2021

Quotes

I've been encouraged and challenged to hear people in our local congregation recite God's Word in a way that captures the heart and mind and stirs the imagination.

—Jimmy Martin
Former General Secretary, International Baptist Convention

Imagine that instead of engaging a select few, people that you might never have expected confidently recite Scripture and bring God's Word alive as it is being presented. I have seen it in an English-speaking international context with many nations gathered and it is wonderful! The approach found in the Art of Leading Scripture Recitations results in a deeper understanding of Scripture, disciples who make disciples, and the church being built up. I strongly endorse it!

—Tim Faulkner
General Secretary, International Baptist Convention

Recitation is a practical way in which we can hide God's word in our hearts as we also share it with the corporate body in worship.

—Sam Dyer
Pastor, River of Life Church, Frankfurt-am-Main, Germany

This book is dedicated to my little family:
Carol, Anne, and Rebecca.

Contents

Foreword

Speaking God's Word to God's people is a supernatural act. God's Word has the power to comfort and heal, correct and challenge, encourage and lift up even the most forlorn of souls. As a pastor, I know how true this is. I speak God's Word on a weekly basis, and it is a task that I take seriously in our international congregation composed of over fifty nationalities. I see how, despite the diversity of people, God's Word brings our church together in a way that only He could choreograph.

Recitation takes this supernatural act a step further. When a reciter steps onto the platform and speaks the very Word of God to his or her church family, a palpable hush falls over the congregation as everyone is ministered to by the unadulterated Word of God going forth from the heart, mind, and soul of the reciter, through his or her mouth, to the congregation. Speaking God's Word to God's people is, indeed, a supernatural act.

A vibrant and healthy recitation ministry brings this privilege to the congregation in a unique and dynamic way. It is unique because very rarely can anyone claim to speak the pure, unaltered Word of God. It is dynamic because it works so powerfully on many levels: in the heart of the reciter, in the one leading the reciter, and in the hearers of the recitation. More people engaging in a recitation ministry will result in many more people opening themselves up to be changed by the Word of God.

Tom has created an unparalleled resource for the local church.

He has done a marvelous job of pioneering this unique and dynamic craft into a ministry that also serves God's vision for His global church—namely, making disciples. This is the task of any church. We define *making disciples* as helping others take a step closer to maturity in Jesus Christ. This means casually engaging our neighbors, coworkers, families, and friends with the good news of Jesus's saving love. I can recall one of our reciters using their desire to practice their recitation as an excuse to share God's Word with their landlady. What a wonderful door recitation opened to that reciter! But discipleship also means establishing and equipping those who are already in the fold. Here is where Tom has developed a truly unique way to establish and equip believers for the task of ministering God's Word to others.

I am so thankful that Tom has written this book, which is designed as a resource for recitation leaders, helping these committed believers to guide others through the process of preparing for and delivering a recitation of scripture. In scripture, discipleship tends to happen when a few key agents come together: God's Word, God's people, Spirit-led prayer, and persevering in these things. All these elements come together in the process of scripture recitation, so that the reciter, the leader, and the congregation all grow in Christlike maturity. The outcome of a recitation is not just a performance or a completed task, but rather a concrete step toward a new and deeper aspect in our relationships with God, both communally and individually.

This book is a jewel for those who treasure God's Word. The prophet Jeremiah delighted in the Word of God, and because of this, he did not just hear the Word; he ate the Word, allowing it to penetrate deeply into his heart! Jeremiah describes his experience of hearing and communicating God's Word to God's people: "When your words came, I ate them; they were my joy and my heart's delight, for I bear your name, LORD God Almighty" (Jeremiah 15:16 NIV). This is what scripture recitation does within those who partake in this wonderful process. May the Lord bless you as you take your first steps on this exciting journey!

Carsten Lotz
Senior Pastor
International Christian Fellowship, Oberursel, Germany

Introduction

Everyone, with few exceptions, can recite scripture. Although it takes work to memorize and practice to understand, it is within the reach of all people. Leading scripture recitations is also within your grasp, and my hope is that this role will resonate with you. Resonance is a concept in physics and the following analogy comes from that discipline. The concept centers on a special case of resonance known as "sympathetic resonance."

When one of two matching tuning forks is struck and begins to vibrate, the other tuning fork will soon vibrate as well. This is sympathetic resonance. The same thing happens with strings. In fact, stringed musical instruments are designed with this principle in mind.

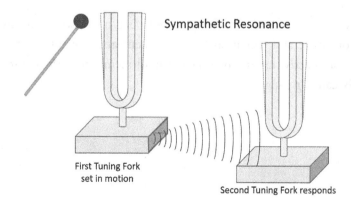

Sympathetic resonance

My hope is that this book will set you in motion to lead others to recite scripture. In this book, you will learn how to plan, develop, and orchestrate a scripture recitation ministry. You'll find checklists, step-by-step processes, troubleshooting tips, guiding principles, and successful, time-proven tactics. Try them out. It may be mechanical at first, but, once set in motion, you may find your resonance. When you do, then you will influence those around you, setting them in motion like that second tuning fork which vibrates because doing so is the natural result of the influence it feels.

If you are a pastor or worship leader, and the result that you desire is for the church to understand scripture, then recitation is one of the methods that will give you success. No amount of "scripture of the week" or "memory verses" even comes close to the depth of understanding participants gain by reciting. And by reciting, they share their insights with those around them. "They read from the Book of the Law of God, *making it clear and giving the meaning* so that the people understood what was being read" (Nehemiah 8:8 NIV, emphasis added).

Recitation is for everyone. It is not intended to be a ministry for an elite group with special skills; neither should it stand alone away from other ministries. It should be incorporated into discipleship groups, Bible studies, youth activities, and mothers' groups, to benefit all.

As you read this book, you will begin to see scripture memorization and recitation as a consistent and valuable part of all worship activities and one in which all members of the church family can participate.

1

The Recitation Leader

Although participants memorize scripture, memorizing scripture is not the primary goal of a recitation ministry. And, although participants study the Bible, a recitation ministry is not solely a Bible study group. Finally, although it is true that participants stand on a stage and speak to an audience, a recitation ministry is also not a Toastmaster's club.

The goal of recitation ministry is more than any of these. It is the live encounter that a reciter experiences through the Holy Spirit as that person shares the truth that he or she has grown to understand from a passage of the Bible. The reciter experiences both sides of the communication equation—hearing the message and speaking it. The reciter becomes intimately close with both the original author of the message as well as its recipients. The purpose of a recitation ministry is to connect people with the message of the Bible personally, to make the written stories, teachings, and praises have heartfelt meanings in the lives of those for whom it was intended. Our vision is to have the Bible communicated accurately and understandably whenever and wherever it is spoken.

Preparing for a recitation is a process of "becoming the message" and being available for the Holy Spirit to work through you. Memorization, focused Bible study, and the mechanics of presentation combine to create a comprehensive and comprehensible message. Diligent pursuit of a passage through repetitive review frequently reveals deeper meaning long after initiating study of it. There is no end to a recitation because you can return to it repeatedly. Each time, there is a new, living interaction. It is a disciplined process full of unexpected benefits.

> "Practicing the memorization discipline is a barometer of my spiritual health. Reviewing a passage over and over reveals meaning one might not have discovered"
>
> —Tim Porter

This book is about the activities and responsibilities of recitation leaders and about making them aware of the possibilities available and the challenges that may arise. It is meant to equip and encourage so that anybody who has a heart to help others will have the tools needed to build a successful recitation ministry.

The Activities of a Recitation Leader

The position of recitation leader is unusual. It is less of a commander and more of a recruiter, scheduler, researcher, encourager, director, and coach. The people whom you lead participate of their own volition, and they can leave at any moment. The recitation plan that you set is simply the one that you devise. You ask people to do the thing that most of them associate with anxiety (i.e., public speaking), while simultaneously requesting that they start with the thing that most people find difficult (i.e., memorizing). Then you have the audacity to request that they act naturally. You will have no leverage to force participation, no carrot to entice activity, and no trophy to capture achievement. You will be utterly at the mercy of the participants. And despite all of that, you will wonder why, after each meeting and rehearsal, you feel less stressed and more alive. You will grow new friendships as you meet and work with people whom you previously didn't know. You will deepen your love of the Word and find the Holy Spirit at work in and around you. It is by no means a thankless job. Indeed, it is a job for which to be thankful.

The activities associated with being a recitation leader are listed below, and we will be elaborating on these in the pages that follow:

- Collaborate with the teaching team to determine suitable passages (Chapter 2).
- Determine the type and elements of the recitation (Chapters 2 and 10).
- Recruit people to recite (Chapter 4).
- Study the passage with the reciters and disciple them (Chapter 5).
- Rehearse and coach reciters in onstage delivery (Chapter 6).
- Ensure the reciter is prepared (Chapter 7).
- Coordinate with the technical and teaching teams (Chapters 8 and 9).
- Support the reciter during the recitation (Chapter 9).
- Ensure that the recitation is documented (Chapter 11).
- Select and prepare visual elements (Chapter 8 and 12).

The Qualities of a Recitation Leader

To be successful, it is essential that a recitation leader possesses or seeks to attain some key qualities. Although there are many qualities that enhance leadership, the three qualities listed below underpin every activity and grease the skids of the recitation toboggan. They are drawn from Moses' words to the Israelites: "The Lord your God will circumcise your hearts and the hearts of your descendants, *so that* you may love him with all your heart and with all your soul, and live" (Deuteronomy 30:6 NIV; emphasis added).

Keep this passage in mind throughout your involvement with recitation in any capacity. The goal, the "so that," is about loving the Lord your God with all your heart and with all your soul. This goal can be achieved even if the recitation isn't perfect or, for that matter, even if the recitation is never delivered.

Encouragement

> "Therefore encourage one another and build up one
> another, just as you also are doing."
> —1 Thessalonians 5:11 (NIV).

For a reciter, the path from agreeing to recite to delivering the recitation can be bumpy. There will be challenges that cause the reciter to doubt him- or herself. It can be a daunting journey. As you guide a reciter, occasionally turn your thoughts back to the first time you were preparing to recite, and this will keep your expectations reasonable. Remember that you can't treat every reciter the same, you must meet them where they are and lift them to the next level. As a leader, you must build up the reciters with honest feedback and encourage them. Honesty and encouragement are not always best friends; however, they can be made to work together. Sometimes, speaking the truth in love means keeping your mouth shut. You will occasionally need to restrain yourself from giving "helpful advice," and instead, focus on what the aspiring reciter is doing right. Reciters need a cheerleader more than they need a critic.

Delight in the Word

> "Blessed is the man who walks not in the counsel of
> the wicked, nor stands in the way of sinners, nor sits
> in the seat of scoffers; but his delight is in the law of
> the LORD, and on his law he meditates day and night."
> —Psalm 1:1–3 (ESV)

If you love to hear the Word of God spoken, then you are in for a treat. As a recitation leader, you will be involved in many rehearsals, in which you will hear the Word recited endlessly. You will spend time grappling with the subtlety of interpretation and probing the depths of understanding the Word. This will be a joy for everybody involved if you genuinely delight in the Word.

Initiative

> "For if anyone is a hearer of the word and not a doer, he is like a man who looks intently at his natural face in a mirror. For he looks at himself and goes away and at once forgets what he was like. But the one who looks into the perfect law, the law of liberty, and perseveres, being no hearer who forgets but a doer who acts, he will be blessed in his doing."
> —James 1:23–25 (NIV)

The beginnings of a recitation are frequently dependent on the leader seeking God's direction and developing a plan that involves a passage of scripture, one or more reciters, the teaching leadership, and a calendar. The leader gets the ball rolling, conspiring with the Holy Spirit to select passages and pair them with people. A recitation doesn't just spontaneously happen. It requires intent and preparation and a spark that gives rise to the fire.

You will draw from and develop these qualities as you help prepare the reciter. In the discipleship model, each member of the group defines goals for themselves. Maybe one of your goals as a leader is to become a better encourager or to take more initiative in service of the Lord. If you feel that you are underdeveloped in any of these necessary leadership qualities, it doesn't mean that you shouldn't lead. On the contrary, it means that you are the best kind of leader—one who realizes his or her own weaknesses and seeks to improve.

2

Initiating a
Recitation Event

"Just as a body, though one, has many parts, but all
its many parts form one body, so it is with Christ."
—1 Corinthians 12:12 (NIV)

Recitation leaders are the driving force in progressing recitation events
and are often also the initiator of the events. It is rare for a recitation
to be initiated by the reciter. The majority of the time, a recitation
is the result of a leader who has chosen a passage, determined the
schedule, recruited the people, and carried it to completion.

Selecting a Passage

The process usually begins with a passage of scripture—but how big
a passage? The answer is that it should be big enough to completely
express at least one concept. For some passages, this can be one verse,
and for others, it may need to be a chapter or more to fully convey
the concept. Our mission is to connect people with the message
of the Bible in conceptually cohesive portions. If a passage is too
small, it risks being done too soon to ever engage the listener. If the
passage is too big, then there is a danger of overloading the audience.

Keep the recitation focused so that it can forge the meaningful connections between people and the biblical message.

If you are targeting a specific Sunday service or event for a recitation, your best source is the pastor or teaching elder. That person will have a concept in mind and can provide guidance on the type of passage that will fit. The pastor will have already thought about how much can be covered reasonably and about the focus of the message.

You should also consider whether the passage will be of benefit to a reciter. It should be a passage that is edifying and that a person would like to have running through his or her head every day for a month or more. Not all passages meet this standard. For example, I would never have someone recite Judges 3:22 (NIV): "Even the handle sank in after the blade, and his bowels discharged. Ehud did not pull the sword out, and the fat closed in over it."

Once you have a passage that conveys a concept, you must decide whether the recitation is meant for one person to deliver or if it is meant for a group to recite.

Selecting a Passage for Individuals

It is good for a person to have a favorite passage that he or she would like to share with others through recitation. This creates a sweet connection between the audience, the passage, and the person because it means sharing one's own life story as that person shares the Word.

However, a recitation ministry will quickly lose life if it depends solely on people reciting passages that they already know and love. There must be a forward drive that challenges one to learn new passages and even to grapple with a style of passage that may be less comfortable to them.

It is important that recitation leaders take the initiative to suggest passages for recitation. If you know someone who has expressed interest in reciting, but this person doesn't have a specific passage in mind, the recitation leader can help in the selection process. Details about how to do this are in chapter four of this book, which covers recruiting.

Selecting a Passage for Groups

Group recitations are a wonderful way to develop relationships in the church family. People who have gone through the process of reciting together establish a bond of shared experience. In addition, it's a great opportunity for communal meals, interactive studies, and fun rehearsals. Don't let the logistics deter you.

When choosing passages for duets, trios, or large groups, consider the following formats:

- Multi-voice recitations
- Multi-language recitations
- Point-counterpoint recitations
- Group Recitations
- Audience participation recitations
- Recitations combined with worship songs

You will find examples of each of these types in this book in chapter three, which covers creative compositions.

Scheduling

If there is any lesson to be learned about recruiting people to recite, it is this: people need a date. The first and second questions from candidates are: "**What** is the passage?" and "**When** will it be recited?" It is much less effective to ask somebody to recite if you don't know when the recitation will take place. You may make broad announcements about reciting, but if you really want to approach someone who has never recited and ask him or her to share a passage, then you should know the date. It is best to have not only a primary date but also a secondary date ready in case there is a scheduling conflict.

It is also important not to rush the reciter. The date needs to be far enough in the future so the person has time to prepare and complete the process. Allow at least a month. I know that some folks can be ready in a couple of days, but you should still allow a month or more.

To know the date, you need to know the teaching calendar and then match the passage to the teaching. It works both ways: either you choose a passage and then see when it will fit the teaching, or you look at the teaching schedule and pick a passage based on it. The critical piece is that there is a schedule of teaching that is set at least a month in the future. This can be a challenge if the teaching schedule is more a seat-of-my-pants-style operation.

The attitude of the pastor or teaching team can make a big difference to scheduling. When recitations are required to be in lockstep with the teaching schedule, then your job as coordinator is greatly more difficult. If, on the other hand, you are given a free hand to select and schedule recitations, then you have the best position for recruiting. At both my former church and my current church, the pastor gave us free reign—and I didn't even have to ask! Both Gary and Carsten, my pastors, told me that there was always a timeslot when a recitation could occur—no obstacles or conditions necessary. They shared the philosophy that hearing the Word is *always* good, and the Holy Spirit can teach from it.

Whether or not there is a teaching schedule, there are three surefire recitation categories that will always be appropriate: psalms of praise, song-related passages, and benedictions. Let's take a look at each of these.

Sure-fire Recitation Categories

Psalms of Praise

Psalms of praise mean any of the psalms that are pure adoration of God, such as Psalm 136, Psalm 117, Psalm 42, or Psalm 56. There isn't a time when these aren't appropriate, so they can always be on the list of passages to recite. Talk to your pastor about the best timing, but I can't imagine any words being more important than these.

Song-Related Passages

Song-related passages are those that are associated with scripture-based songs. For example, the song "Nothing but the Blood" goes with 1 John 1:7, Hebrews 10:19–22, Isaiah 1:18, and Psalm 51:7. If your worship team includes this song in its repertoire, then you have four possible recitations. Hymns are replete with scripture, as are many modern songs. Look at Charlie Hall's song "Center" and find all the scripture references, or the song "How He Loves" by the David Crowder Band. If you ask someone to recite passages from these songs, and these worship songs fit into your worship team's repertoire, then you just need to find out when the team will be including that song in the order of worship. Hearing the Word spoken and sung is both inspiring and instructive.

Benedictions

I think that the concept of a benediction (which literally means "good word") comes from the feeling that worshipping together makes it heartbreaking to say good-bye, and the benediction serves as the embrace before parting. Numerous passages can serve as this final embrace such as Numbers 6:22–26, Romans 15:5–6, 1 Corinthians 15:58, or Ephesians 3:17–19. There are many, and any one of them could fit on any Sunday. This is something for which you can take the initiative and have several reciters prepared with encouraging and thoughtful "good words."

3

Creative Compositions

The most common form of recitation involves one person reciting one passage in one language. There are, however, more ways of presenting a recitation that also highlight the depth, diversity, consistency, and beauty of the Word.

Tap into your creative side to compose a nontraditional recitation that involves multiple people, multiple languages, or multiple passages. This chapter is meant to provide you with some examples to whet your appetite. There are certainly more creative minds that will weave together passages as the Spirit leads.

Take special care to not lose the intended meaning of the passage(s) as you create your recitation. Joining together short clips of verses, taken out of context and put into a montage, is a danger to avoid. Seriously study your recitation composition and apply the disciplined study of the message that is described in chapter five of this book. Seek wise counsel to provide feedback and to employ the review cycles that every recitation should undergo.

The following sections describe a variety of recitation formats. Each section includes a synopsis of an example. Complete scripts for many of these recitations are available for download on the By Heart website, found at https://ByHeart.org. Some example scripts can also be found in Appendix IV of this book.

Multi-Voice Recitations

Although it is only a small variation from a solo recitation, a single passage recited by two, three, or more voices keeps the listener engaged. The personalities of the reciters provide ready-made dynamics. Following are two examples of multi-voice recitations.

John 1:1–18: The Word Became Flesh

This passage sounds like it was intended to be spoken by two voices! There is a complementarity between the parts that propels this recitation, and you may find the two reciters interacting naturally as they "pass the ball" back and forth.

Daniel 3:1–18: Rebuff Nebuchadnezzar

The composition that we did was divided into three voices and was intended to have a light feel with rapid changes between the reciters, keeping it fun—until the final three verses, when things get very serious, very quickly: "King Nebuchadnezzar, we do not need to defend ourselves before you in this matter. If we are thrown into the blazing furnace, the God we serve is able to deliver us from it, and he will deliver us from Your Majesty's hand. But even if he does not, we want you to know, Your Majesty, that we will not serve your gods or worship the image of gold you have set up" (Daniel 3:16–18 NIV).

Multi-Language Recitations

The more international your audience, the more you will want to consider multilingual recitations. The language with which people think, pray, and meditate is their "heart language," and it is not English for everyone. For someone who is living outside of his or her native language country, it can be a wonderful blessing to hear scripture in his or her native language. This holds true for all spoken languages, as well as for non-spoken languages. We had a fabulous recitation in which the prime language was American Sign Language, and the translation was into English.

Multi-lingual Pentecost

This group recitation is also multilingual and has verses that are interspersed with Acts 2:1–12. The non-English language reciters present their verses in both their non-English languages as well as in English. After the first reciter completes Acts 2:1–4, all the reciters join onstage and there is a "murmur" of all the languages being recited at once. During this time, the first reciter continues with Acts 2:5–9. Then, each reciter goes in turn, first in the non-English language, and then in English. The passages in this recitation are:

- Acts 2:1–12,
- Isaiah 60:19,
- Psalm 19:1,
- Psalm 65:8, and
- Psalm 31:21.

A Two-Language Recitation

When reciting in two languages, it is livelier to do a real-time translation, rather than having one reciter do the entire passage and then the other reciter reciting the entire passage. A real-time translation breaks the passage into smaller bites with the speakers alternating phrase-by-phrase. If doing this, it is best to minimize the dead air space, that is, the time between one speaker and the other. In fact, overlapping the phrases by a small amount keeps the momentum of the passage going. You can find a good example of this in the 1 Corinthians 9:19-23 script found in Appendix IV of this book.

Point-Counterpoint Recitations

The Juxtaposition of Man's Way (Romans 3:9–17) and God's Way (Psalm 18:30–33)

This recitation puts the nature of God and the nature of man in opposition. This example is in two languages, so there is a tension between both language and content as the recitation switches from a complete presentation of Romans 3:9–17 (the nature of man), in German,[1] to a point-counterpoint presentation of both passages in English, and then concludes with the complete passage of Psalm 18:30–33, describing the beauty of God.

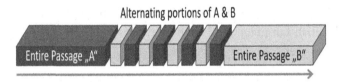

Diagram representing the composition structure.

The diagram illustrates the general composition of this recitation, beginning with passage A—the presentation of man's way (Romans 3:10–17)—and ending with passage B, the beauty of God (Psalm 18:30–33). In between, the reciters seem to spar with each other as they alternate phrases of their passages.

Group Recitations

Group recitations are a wonderful way to develop relationships in a church body by having a shared experience. Combining people who may not typically interact by involving them in a group recitation will foster interaction among the group members and open new

---

[1] Römer 3, verse 9 bis 17 übersetzt von Hermann Menge unveränderter Nachdruck der 11. Auflage, ©1949. Württembergische Bibelanstalt Stuttgart.

avenues of communication and new relationships. Gather inter-generational groups, people of varying socio-economic categories, introverts and extroverts, and leaders and followers; the benefits of your intentional diversity when selecting members for a group recitation will strengthen your community.

The discipleship aspect of a recitation comes to the forefront in a group recitation. The group will study the passage together and derive the intended meaning. This knowledge will inform the way that they deliver the message. Together, your diverse group will be discussing the Word together and sharing insights. They will have the opportunity to interact in a way that they never may have previously. Your group recitation will have facilitated this.

Group recitations, however, are rarely easy to produce. The most difficult task is coordinating schedules. Although I have no magic solution, I can tell you that coordinating group recitations became much easier when I quit arranging the recitation schedule around everybody else's schedule and, instead, just told them what the recitation schedule would be and asked that they adjust their schedules to accommodate.

Father's Day Advice

This recitation starts by turning the tables. Five children provide advice to fathers, giving little jewels of encouragement and counsel, with a touch of self-serving advice. Then, as would be expected, five fathers provide wisdom to their children. The passages start with the reciter providing a summary of their advice and then reciting the scripture that illustrates this advice. For example, Kyla said, "Be kind" and then recited Psalm 103:3 (NIV): "As a father shows compassion to his children, so the Lord shows compassion to those who fear him." There were some humorous moments as the advice from the kids tended to be self-serving, such as Ephesians 6:4 (NIV), "Fathers, do not exasperate your children …" and Proverbs 13:22 (ESV), "A good man leaves an inheritance to his children's children ..." but there wasn't a dry eye in the audience when our youngest participant recited the essence of the prodigal son from Luke 15:20 (NIV), when the father drops everything and runs to greet his wayward son: "His father saw him and was filled with compassion for him; he ran to his son, threw his arms around him and kissed him."

Psalm 51 in Nine Languages

An international church provides plenty of opportunities for multilingual recitations. When we did the Psalm 51 recitation, it was remarkable—more than in the diversity of languages, it was the diversity of ages and social groups represented in the nine participants that was most heart-warming: a retired French lady with a tragic past, side-by-side with a young man from Brazil who was just finishing his university entrance qualification; the Croatian data analyst collaborating with the young financial consultant from Hong Kong. They discussed the rhythm and tone of languages and were united around this beautiful psalm of confession.

In delivering the recitation, it would have been too long and repetitive to quote each verse in every language, so the script was composed to distribute verses to each language, and then there were some portions in which everybody recited together in one language.

True Religion

This three-person recitation is focused on those acts that are unquestionably good and right, and that weave together three passages:

- Deuteronomy 10:14–19,
- Isaiah 1:11–12 and 1:15b–17, and
- James 1:26–27.

The Quilt

The quilt recitation is more than a recitation because intrinsic to it are interactions between the teaching leader and the reciters. It is an opportunity for great fellowship within a group of reciters, and each reciter can bring his or her unique personal connections and insights. It begins with everyone, in turn, reciting one of his or her passages. All the passages are short (one to two verses), and each reciter has at least two passages assigned. After the complete run-through, then the teaching elder or pastor does a brief interview with each person that involves him or her reciting the passage again and then describing something significant, either in the passage itself or as it relates to the reciter's life.

The passages involved in this recitation are:

- Deuteronomy 30:19–20a
- Joshua 1:9
- 1 Timothy 4:12
- Micah 6:8
- Romans 12:2
- Philippians 1:4–6
- Matthew 5:16
- Romans 12:9–10
- 2 Timothy 1:7
- Luke 6:35

Audience Participation Recitations

Acts 3:1–4:20

In what can only be described only as "experimental," this passage was recited using human "props" from the audience to play the characters in the passage: Peter, John, and a man crippled from birth, Annas (the high priest), and members of the high priest's family. The reciter not only recites the passage but also prompts and positions the characters onstage. A helper can assist with providing attire for the human props.

19

The Attributes of God

Attributes of God is an audience-participation game involving scripture. The audience is presented with a list of attributes of God, ideally projected on a screen, but printed on a page works, as well. Then a passage is recited. The question to the audience is, "Which attribute of God did this passage describe?" The catch is that, almost without exception, the attribute is not explicitly mentioned in the passage.

Run a ten-second countdown clock and then reveal the answer. If the reciter has a comment about the attribute, this would be a good time to share it.

One or two is enough for a day. You can spread the game over several weeks. Below are the attributes that we used and the verses for each attribute. There are many more verses that match the attributes; these show just one example.

Attribute of God	Passage
Immense	1 Kings 8:27 Isaiah 66:1
Infinite	Psalm 36:5–6 Job 36:26
Good	Matthew 7:9–11
Perfect	Psalm 19:7–11
Just	Psalm 9:7–8
Holy	Isaiah 6:4–5
Omnipresent	Psalm 139:7–12
Omniscient	Psalm 139:1–6
Immanent	Isaiah 7:14
Graceful	Romans 5:8
Merciful	Psalm 103:8–18 2 Peter 3:9 Ezekiel 33:11

Recitations combined with Worship Songs

This form of recitation places the scripture recitation amid a worship song. More common is to recite a scripture either before or after a worship song, but, in this case, the scripture is mixed together with the song.

We have used the songs "How He Loves," written by John Mark McMillan, and "Center," written by Charlie Hall and Matt Redman, for this type of recitation. These songs are especially good because they are both so rich with scriptural references.

When preparing for these recitations, it takes some time to work with the musicians to place the recitations in the song and work out the timing. It helps if your reciters have some feel for rhythm because their entrance and pace must match the song's.

Holy Day Recitations

Good Friday

This Good Friday series of recitations is taken from Mark chapters 14 and 15, plus one passage from Isaiah 53. Between the passages, worship songs are played. The worship song begins either just as the passage ends or overlaps with a few notes as the passage is concluding. After the last passage is recited, the congregation is invited to exit quietly.

- Mark 14:1–11
- Mark 14:12–16
- Mark 14:27–50
- Mark 14:53–65
- Isaiah 53:2–8
- Mark 14:66–72
- Mark 15:1–20
- Mark 15:21–37

Christmas Prophecy Fulfilled

A series of recitations of prophecy are related to the birth of Christ and then the fulfillment of the prophecies in Christ. In our presentation, we interspersed carols and worship songs between these prophecies. We used seven reciters with each reciting two or three passages. It is also possible to intersperse readings in this presentation of prophecy and fulfillment at Christmas.

Tribute Recitations

When a family is departing after years of service, or someone has achieved a milestone in his or her life, or there is a group award or achievement, it is fitting to take time to pay tribute to the people involved. If we are honest, however, at tributes there can be a tendency for the people paying tribute to slip into well-meaning but repetitive phrases. For example, "Rodger always has a smile and a friendly greeting" or "Laurie is always ready to help." These phrases may be heartfelt and well-intended, but they fall short of elegant expression.

A solution to this is a tribute recitation, which gives meaningful content to people who would like to express their appreciation and provide encouragement. In a tribute recitation, participants are given a passage of scripture that has been personalized for the honoree. In these passages, the first-person pronouns are replaced with the name of the honoree. For example, "But thanks be to God, who always leads *Carol* in triumph in Christ, and reveals through *Carol* the sweet aroma of His knowledge in every place" (2 Corinthians 2:14 WEB, emphasis added).[2]

Not only are first-person pronouns replaced with a name, but second- and third-person pronouns are adjusted to match the gender, and there are occasionally adjustments that need to be made based

---

[2] World English Bible translation from http://www.yourpersonalizedbible.com.

on marital status. The idea is to make both the selected passage, and the delivery of the passage, personal. Here is another example: "No longer do I call Jeff a servant, for a servant doesn't know what his lord does. But I have called Jeff a friend, for everything that I heard from My Father, I have made known to Jeff" (John 15:15 WEB, emphasis added).

Tributes tend to be emotional, and the combination of reciting from memory and being too "choked up" to speak is not a good one. A good solution for this is to record a video of the tribute. A video also gives something tangible to the honoree(s).

Extending the video approach, the *location* of the personalized recitation may also be personalized. One tribute that we did was for the caretaker at our church. He had served faithfully in a wide range of capacities. We recorded videos in places that he, in years to come, would remember as having been significant to him: the boiler room, beside the cantankerous dishwasher, the storage room, and his workshop.

4

Recruiting

When recruiting people to recite, you act as the matchmaker who matches a passage with a person and a date. The rationale for your match, the reason that you linked this person with that passage, will help you to encourage a person to recite.

The process happens in one of two ways. It either starts with a plan that you have, and for which you will find people, or it starts with a person who has a desire to recite but doesn't have a specific passage in mind.

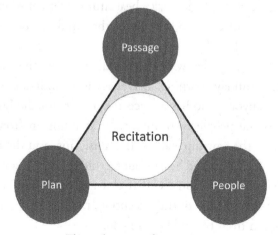

Three elements of a recitation

Either way, you play the matchmaker, putting together people with passages in the context of a plan.

Matchmaking

The match is between a voice and a message. My favorite story about matchmaking was with an encouraging passage from Jeremiah: "'For I know the plans I have for you,' declares the LORD, 'plans to prosper you and not to harm you, plans to give you hope and a future. Then you will call on me and come and pray to me, and I will listen to you'" (Jeremiah 29:11–12 NIV).

The comforting voice of the Lord encourages his people—but what does the voice of the Lord *sound* like? I struggle with passages in which the creator of the universe is given voice and I wanted to avoid the cliché, booming male voice of God. My deliberation ended when I realized that the important quality of the voice was not its power, but, rather, its purity. The voice for this passage would need to penetrate doubts and defenses with a clear and authentic message of hope.

Charlotte ("Lottie"), the ten-year-old young lady who recited that passage, conveyed the purity beautifully. Her benediction was as close to the voice of God as any of the hundreds of people she blessed had ever heard.

When you consider who you should recruit, then just look around on a Sunday morning. *Everybody* is a candidate, with few exceptions. Anyone who has a voice and a heart for the Lord. One exception is the people who are always standing in front of the congregation: the worship leaders, the musicians, and the teachers. They truly have voices and hearts, but recruiting them just reinforces the idea that recitation is an exclusive club and only a few people can recite scripture. Outside of this exception, the ripe fields are sitting next to you, in front of, and behind you.

Oftentimes, those people around you are reluctant to

volunteer—but they *want* to be asked. So, ask. What's the worst that can happen? Yes, you will need to get familiar with the occasional rejection, but you will also be surprised at how frequently the person you ask will already have been considering participating. They just needed to be asked. So, take the initiative, approach them, and ask.

The Key Question

When recruiting a reciter, there is one key question that cuts to the heart of the matter. This question is phrased in a way that assumes the person wants to recite, and now the decision is about the topic of the recitation. The question propels the decision forward, helping to narrow the range of possibilities and make the prospect of reciting tangible. Best of all, instead of being some cleverly devised trick that persuades somebody against his or her will, this question is straightforward and puts the person in charge of making the decision. Keeping the reciter in charge is a key principle in working with reciters, and it is an appropriate way to get the journey started.

The question is:

Would you be interested in reciting a story, a teaching, or a praise?

Pose that question to your candidate, and chat about the possibilities. You will be helping your soon-to-be reciter to envision his or her recitation and will be getting this person to think about the message that he or she wants to convey. The question respects the person. It is persuasive without cajoling or pressuring.

The question contains three categories: story, teaching, or praise. You may want to further divide the categories to explain the nature of each, as I've done below.[3]

---

[3] For specific passages that fit these categories, please refer to the Appendix of our companion book *The Art of Reciting Scripture*.

- Story (Narratives)
  - o Acts of faith
  - o Prophecy

- Teaching
  - o Admonishment and worldly influence
  - o Christian walk

- Praise
  - o God's love for us
  - o Person and deity of Christ
  - o Praise

The categorization is simple, and that is its beauty. You, being the smart person that you are, may already have picked out some exceptions to these categories. However, when someone is considering participating in a recitation, it is easier to ask whether he or she would like to recite "a story, a teaching, or a praise" than it is to leave it open-ended.

The Recitation Opportunity Card

It's an electronic age; however, when it comes to confirming a recitation, get it on paper. We can all be forgetful. What was the verse? What was the date? What is it that I said I would do? If it's written down, then all the uncertainties are laid to rest.

I have a formal card that I sometimes give out, which helps everyone involved. Of course, I often forget the card—but I still write it down. A napkin, the backside of a pamphlet, a receipt—it all works. Just make it easy for the reciter to have an unambiguous reference. What seems so obvious and memorable at the start can become a jumbled array of numbers and names over time. If the person you are recruiting agrees to recite, then give him or her a card like this one. It doesn't have to be this pretty, but it should have this information:

A recitation opportunity card.

And don't forget a note to yourself. Lately, I've been taking a picture of the person holding the reference card. This way it is easy for me to connect the person, passage, and date.

Counteracting Excuses

Linda had a desire to recite, and she devoted much time to memorizing scripture. She always attended the "open mic" recitation evenings, stood up front, and recited. I would follow her words using the handwritten 3×5 cards she had written on, front and back, with cursive letters in blue ink or even in pencil. The cards were smudged and dog-eared. Some words were underlined; others were crossed out and rewritten. The cards themselves told a story of diligent effort. When Linda recited, she was exuberant in her gestures and voice. She wasn't "acting," but rather, she was being exactly who she is. Her love for our Lord and the Word is genuine and delightful. Her love of reciting has an added dimension because she has been diagnosed with a form of dementia, like Alzheimer's disease, and memorizing scripture is one weapon that she uses in her fight back against this ruthless enemy.

So, if a mature lady fighting dementia can recite, then who can't? Who can say "I have such a bad memory"? Most of the excuses that people have are, from a different perspective, exactly the reasons that they should be involved in a recitation.

- Bad memory? That is a great reason *to recite*. Memory must be exercised to get better, and a bad memory is a reason to exercise.
- Afraid of public speaking? You will never find a better audience than your church family. We are all rooting for you and will love you no matter how you do onstage.
- Not an actor? Perfect. We want people to be themselves— nothing more, and nothing less.

Granted, for some people, verbatim recitation is very difficult. For many, the prospect of speaking to a large audience strikes fear in their hearts. However, I've known a few people who had no problem being in front of people and speaking, but they did have a problem— it was their skill in *improvising*! They were so good at thinking on their feet and coming up with quick responses that they tended to go "off book" and invent things when they couldn't remember the exact words. This is a nightmare scenario for a recitation leader because it is hard to get somebody back on track when he or she has taken a completely different train!

Nevertheless, I've heard these excuses, and I would, instead, prefer to focus on the positives, the reasons that one should recite. There are solid arguments for participating in a recitation. You may have your own list; here is mine:

Top Ten Reasons to Recite

1. Because you have a bad memory (it's a muscle that should be exercised).
2. It's a biblical command (Deuteronomy 11:18–21).
3. It will help you to overcome your fear of public speaking.
4. You will be prepared to share the Word with others.
5. You will become a better communicator.
6. You will get to know more people in your church family.
7. Your church family will get to know you.
8. You will be a contributor.
9. You will be a witness to those around you.
10. It is the best Bible study ever, and it will forever change how you study the Bible.

The Hard Reality

As you attempt to recruit people, you will probably become familiar with rejection. People will avert their eyes so as not to make eye-contact with you. They will sidestep around your path. Soon, you will be able to recognize the various phrases that mean no. For example, "I'll think about it" means no; "I'll need to check my schedule" means no; and "You should ask Joe" means no. As you try to coordinate schedules, you will wonder if there is someone behind the scenes, maliciously orchestrating the perfect misalignment of availabilities. Do not lose heart. All you can do is to present opportunities. Your role isn't to force anybody to do anything. It is no more possible to force someone to recite than it is to throw a Ping-Pong ball to the moon.

Not only is it impossible to force someone to recite, you shouldn't want to. The benefit and overwhelming blessing of recitation is between the reciter and the Lord. The benefit to the reciter is the determined involvement of the Holy Spirit to reveal truth, taking words that didn't make sense or that were understood at a superficial level, and resolving them into spiritual understanding. This only happens during those weeks of preparation as the reciter grapples with the Word during a personal journey that they

Keep the reciter in charge of the recitation from the very start.

have willingly entered. Manipulating people or positions to get some result is a fool's approach and only succeeds in dodging the blessing.

As you recruit reciters, you are the catalyst who makes it easier for people to participate. The Holy Spirit is already at work in these people's lives. You are simply providing them with specific opportunities. It can feel like a daunting task and you may need to get out of your own comfort zone as you reach out in this role as matchmaker. Despite the excuses and hard reality that you may face, there will be scores of people who will be grateful that you asked, that you boldly approached them with a passage and a date.

5

Recitation Discipleship

Once you have the person and the passage, then the prep begins. The best way to proceed is not to send that person off into the woods to memorize alone; it is better to come alongside him or her with a group of allies, a discipleship group. The goal of a discipleship group is to encourage each other forward to maturity in Christ.

Discipleship propels us along the path to being conformed to the image of Christ (Romans 8:29) and breathes life into our encounters with the Word. That is the big picture. With recitation, however, it is easy to get bogged down in the fine minutiae and forget the big picture. We worry about memorizing the correct pronouns, which words to emphasize, and when we should pause. We repeat phrases over and over, trying to get the correct intonation. By its nature, recitations cause us to become very detail oriented. Although these details are important in composing a clear message, don't lose sight of the fact that the primary goal of this discipline is not to put on a good show, but to grow the spiritual maturity of the reciter.

It would be a shame to have a flawless recitation and no growth. The recitation is the vehicle to a deeper understanding of the scripture and drives every relationship, both the heartfelt and the heavy, with buddies and bullies alike. A recitation is a means to reach into the church family and encourage each person to contribute to the growth and development of everyone in the community.

In your capacity as a recitation leader, you will be investing in the life of the reciter to help clarify his or her priorities and to make decisions about how he or she behaves in his or her relationships. The preparation for a recitation is a preparation that applies to every relationship and reaches beyond the reciter to everyone connected to that person.

Charity is a friend and member of my church. She has delivered multiple recitations, and each time, she finds some new opportunity for growth because she knows that the recitation is a vehicle to move her along as a disciple. Listen to the outward focus from Charity: "Recitation is about God being at work in the reciter, changing and preparing me to be a vessel to carry His word out to others." She understands that the recitation is meant for those she holds in relationship as much as it is for herself. To join with someone in a recitation-discipling relationship is one of the best gifts that you can give. It means that you are willing to invest in him or her. The result will not only benefit the reciter and all who hear the recitation, but it will also benefit his or her relationships and future studies. Let's walk through the stages of a discipleship group to see how you can equip the group members and also be nourished yourself.

Stage One: Building Trust

The starting point for the discipleship group will be establishing your trust connections and defining where each person is in his or her spiritual development. You may feel that, as the leader, you are meant to have all the answers. You're not. Each person is on his or her own journey—and so are you. In this portion of the discipleship, be sure to establish expectations from everybody. This is your agreement to participate with specific goals and levels of commitment. As with all discipleship, your goal is to progress the others along their path of becoming disciples of Christ. At some point along the way, the disciples will become the disciple leaders. You are serving as a model for them.

There are four foundations at the core of the covenant with the reciter. These are:

1. The reciter chooses the version of the passage that he or she will recite.[4]
2. The reciter will be given enough time to prepare.
3. The reciter will be supported when reciting.
4. The reciter has the final say on when he or she recites.

Both the reciter and the recitation leader make a commitment of time and effort. Get this agreement out in the open and even record it on paper. Specific commitments from both the leader and the reciter sets clear expectations and avoids disappointments.

Stage Two: Understanding

Recitation is not possible without learning the words and grasping what they *mean*. This stage begins the infusion of understanding into the passage so that when the reciter is speaking, there will be clarity of communication.

The recitation ministry is unique in many ways, including how we go about studying the Bible. There is an intentionality in each step of our process that points to the recitation. We study the passage so that we can accurately convey the message.

We study with a focus on the moment that the words came to life. This includes the background of the writer and the audience, their relationship, the culture, the circumstances of the writing, and the intention of its delivery. We study to learn the context of the passage so that we can faithfully reanimate it. As such, a Bible study

---

[4] Reciters should pick the version as long as it's a translation and not an interpretation.

in preparation for a recitation has a certain bent, leaning toward origins rather than extrapolations, toward what caused it rather than what it will cause.

The following table seeks to compare the intentions of a traditional Bible study with a recitation Bible study:

Traditional Bible Study	Recitation Bible Study
Understand how to apply the passage in our daily lives	Understand what *prompted* the publication of the passage in the first place
Explore the range of possible meanings of a passage	Decide on the *one* tone and texture of the passage that will be recited
Define the syntax of the words of the passage	Define how the words of the passage will be voiced
Identifying word etymology to understand connections to other passages	Identifying word prompts and cues that will trigger recall

A recitation Bible study analyzes the passage through four perspectives: participants, tone, relationships, and tempo. The participants are those characters on both sides of the communication; the tone describes the force and inflection of the sound of the words, which is informed by the relationship between the participants; the selection and definition of the words are the core of the communication; and the tempo matches the rhythm of speech with the intent of the providing punctuation and pattern to the reciter.

Leading the Analysis

The intent of the passage must be understood before a recitation can be of any value. We have a responsibility to present just what the scripture says in a way that conveys the original intent. There is a danger of misinterpretation, and leaders must be aware of and be able to rectify this, should it arise. Even if the words are accurate, a reciter may still convey a meaning that is not aligned with the original intent due to his or her body language, tone, or tempo. Some of the misinterpretation can be grammatically based. If I described the actions of an object that "eats shoots and leaves" versus "eats, shoots, and leaves," is it a koala bear or a hunter? More often, however, the confusion arises from the subtleties that color a communication.

The nuance that can be conveyed in a recitation is both the beauty and the danger. A shoulder shrug, a sideways glance, a hesitation—there are just so many ways to convey meaning that either align with and reinforce the words and the intent of the message, or that present an inaccurate interpretation. That is why this portion of the preparation, the understanding of the intent, is critical. It will also be ongoing as you continue to revisit this during rehearsals and re-evaluate the interpretations.

Stage Three: Synthesis

In the synthesis stage, the understanding that has been gleaned is assimilated and externalized. There is a parallel between applying the learning to a reciter's recitation and applying the learning to the reciter's life. Get it right onstage, and maybe you can get it right in life. Yes, it is only one presentation, but I think that people understand this link. We all have the feeling that we are being watched and evaluated. This is true more often than we care to admit; especially as Christians, it is a fact of life that our lives are being scrutinized.

Synthesis involves clarifying the message through rehearsals and revisions. It requires care about details and paying attention to how the passage is expressed so that it aligns with the original intent. As you coach a reciter, you will be in a position to promote practices that are not only needed for the recitation, but that can also be valuable life skills: discipline, perseverance, courage, and concentration.

Stage Four: Discipling others

Discipleship multiplies disciples. Once a person has been through the process of selection, preparation, and delivery of a recitation, he or she is a step closer to being the one to lead others on this journey. In leading a reciter, you are also developing a future leader. The way in which you guide a reciter may result in not only a good recitation, but also a reciter who is better equipped to lead others through the process.

It is worth your time as the recitation leader to let the reciter know what is happening behind the scenes. Describe how you are communicating with the pastor, the sound crew, the translators, and the music team. As often as possible, put the reciter in charge of a decision so that he or she can weigh the factors involved in ensuring the message is delivered accurately, clearly, and with a focus on exalting our Savior. In doing so, you are not only helping this person appreciate the moment, but you are also preparing him or her for a chance to take the reins in the future as a leader.

6

Rehearsal

As early and as often as possible, the reciter should be reciting onstage. Speaking while onstage is not something that most people do every day. It can be unfamiliar territory and there may be some anxiety. As a recitation leader, it is important that you have driven this road yourself and understand how fraught it can be with hazards. Your assurances and encouragement to a reciter are empty if you have never prepared for a recitation yourself. Your guidance is just book knowledge unless you have struggled through the uncertainties and faced the fears yourself.

We all need practice with being on a stage, speaking out loud, and getting accustomed to the vantage point. It is okay to start practicing even if the entire passage is not yet memorized. In fact, you should encourage reciters to get onstage early—as soon as they have at least one section of the passage ready. They need to get acquainted with stage motions (i.e., "blocking"), boundaries, and obstacles. Help reciters to feel comfortable onstage so that it is a source of strength to them instead of intimidation. Help them use that vantage point as a place that embraces them with memory clues and tailor their motions to be in tune with their surroundings. You need to help reciters turn the stage from foreign turf into friendly ground.

Blocking

The term *blocking* refers to the movements of a reciter onstage during the recitation. Every move he or she makes (e.g., walking across the stage, climbing stairs, sitting in a chair, getting down on bended knee) falls under the larger term called *blocking*.

But what is the purpose of blocking when it comes to recitation?

1. **To engage the audience**. We can't lose sight of the fact that a reciter is typically speaking to many people at once. The trick is to make each person in the audience feel like, at some point, you are talking directly to him or her. We try to convey that intimacy by engaging sections of the audience intently for a brief time. Our rule of thumb is eight seconds. For eight seconds, the reciter will look and speak directly to a person in one section of the audience. After that time, his or her gaze moves and eventually settles on another person in another section. In a one-minute[5] recitation, the reciter can focus on six different sections, and that makes the audience feel like they have been included.

2. **To assist with memory**. One of the memory techniques presented in our companion book, *The Art of Reciting Scripture*, is termed "Focus Progression," and it depends on creating a correlation between where the reciter is looking and which portion of the passage is being recited. Developing this relationship reinforces both the motions and aids memory.

3. **To change roles**. If a passage contains multiple voices, then reciters may want to reposition when changing roles. From changing the direction of their gaze to walking across the stage, there is a huge range of repositioning that will help

[5] Recitations typically last between 45 seconds and two minutes

the audience understand that a change in the conversation is happening.[6]

4. **To change tone.** A movement can make an emphasis or clarify a concept, but here we come to the boundary of acting and reciting. As a recitation leader, you need to continually evaluate whether reciters are expressing themselves naturally or whether they are making gestures that are forced. As soon as a reciter is no longer expressing him- or herself in a way that is consistent with his or her typical behavior, you need to throw up the red flag. The boundary is different for each person, so there is no way to codify this. It is up to your judgment in collaboration with the reciter. Remember, we are asking reciters to express themselves naturally in a situation that is clearly not natural— that is, standing on a stage in front of hundreds of people. You will need to work with them to bring them to who they naturally are. I have many stories about very animated people who freeze up and become mannequins, or about quiet people who take on a "stage persona" and become something that they usually are not. Getting somebody to be him- or herself while onstage is one of the biggest challenges in reciting.

5. **To remind reciters about body language.** We block a recitation so that the reciter remembers that his or her physical motions convey information and that we must be tuned in to that message and align it with the words.

Tone

If you've been scolded for bad behavior, or comforted when you were sad, or carefully guided through a difficult problem, then you

---

[6] See chapter 10 "Onstage Techniques" in the companion book, *The Art of Reciting Scripture*

understand about the importance of the tone of voice in the person speaking to you.

Consider your passage of Scripture. What is the tone of the message? Is the tone consistent, or does it change over the course of the passage?

The decision of tone is foundationally important and much of what you do in this phase of animation will depend on your choice. The tone must make sense in light of the words and what you understand as well as with the purpose of the message.

Types of Expression

Facial expressions can break your heart, cheer you up, or make you doubt. Just because an audience seems far away, doesn't mean that they won't see a raised eyebrow or a slight grimace onstage. Encourage your reciter to consider these details. More often than not, the reciter is not aware of distracting or inconsistent expression.

Similarly, hand motions can convey meaning—but, if you don't know what to do with them, leave your hands at your sides. Granted, some people would become mute if they were not allowed to move their hands, but hand motions can have drawbacks. My favorite hand-motion story involved a speaker who would rub his hands together in a way that reminded me of a huckster. After seeing him do it consistently, I mentioned that he may want to change his hand position to something that looked a little more thoughtful and less conniving. He took this advice to heart. Years later, he became a pastor and was never accused of being a huckster.

A Typical Rehearsal Agenda

The rehearsal is primarily the reciter onstage running through the passage, but there are some other components. A typical rehearsal looks like this:

- Ten minutes: Pray and talk about the passage one-to-one while seated.
- Five minutes: First run-through of the passage onstage.
- Ten minutes: Run through the passage again—with interruptions for comments.
- Fifteen minutes: Discuss pauses, words to emphasize, and transitions.
- Twenty minutes: Run through the passage onstage (repeatedly).
  - After each run-through, the leader should bring up some of the following points:
    - Did the reciter address the entire audience?
    - Did the reciter incorporate pauses and vary the tempo?
    - Was there vocal variety?
    - Was the blocking effective?
    - How was the information from the Bible study used?
    - What looked awkward?
- Five minutes: Wrap up with expectations for the next session.

Common Mistakes to Identify in Rehearsal

As a recitation leader, you will need to provide gentle correction. If you bring these points up before the rehearsal really gets moving, then you will be more of a coach and less of a nag. Get ahead of these:

- **Tailing off.** Sometimes, the reciter's volume tends to drop near the end of a sentence. It is a common error when speaking in public. Make your reciters aware of the tendency for "tailing off" and work to counteract it. Many times, the last words of a sentence are the most critical to the overall meaning of the message and dropping them can leave the audience with an incorrect understanding.

- **Wandering onstage.** Whether pacing or drifting, stage motions draw attention. If the motion is planned and supports the message, then it is great. If it is random, accidental, or mindless, then it is distracting. Every motion onstage should be planned and aligned with the message. There is also a safety factor here. There are frequently cables and other obstacles onstage. Wandering can lead to stumbling and tripping. We don't want anyone to get hurt.

- **Awkward hands.** When left alone, people's hands help them to communicate—some more than others. But when people start to think about their hands, that's when the hands can become a problem. I used to be more prescriptive in addressing the question of "What do I do with my hands?" until I realized that the hands were not the problem—the problem was that the reciter hadn't yet internalized the passage. When the reciter "owns" the passage, then the rest of their body will join in with the communication. Yes, it can help to suggest some different hand positions and let the reciters decide if these fit the way they naturally communicate—but the best answer to the question of body language is to develop a more intimate understanding of the passage. If reciters can't be natural, then ask them to leave their hands at their sides. It is better that they do nothing with their hands than to "play charades" during a recitation.

- **Talking too fast.** If a reciter speaks too quickly, then the audience doesn't have a chance for the words to sink in. The audience doesn't know what the reciter is going to say, so slow the reciter down. One problem is anxiety. If the reciter is nervous, it is likely that he or she will speak too quickly. The other common problem is lack of familiarity with the passage. If the reciter does not know the passage well enough, then he or she is likely to rush through it before it "leaks out" of his or her brain again. Both anxiety and rushing are symptoms that stem from a lack of understanding and connection with the passage. As a leader, you may need to remind the reciter to slow down; but, more importantly, you need to help the reciter understand the significance and impact of the message he or she is delivering. When this happens, then the reciter slows down. In short, don't just press down on the brakes—understand the reason that the train is running out of control in the first place.

On-Book

The person "on-book" makes sure that the reciter has a memory prompt if the reciter loses their place or forgets the next word. During a recitation, the person on-book will be in the front row of the audience with the text in front of him or her, ready to support the reciter. The on-book person's task is to follow the text word for word. If the reciter pauses, then the on-book person should look up. If the reciter is pausing for dramatic effect, then the on-book person should not intervene. If, however, the reciter is looking directly at the on-book person, then that person should call out the next two or three words in a loud voice. The goal is to get the reciter back on track. As the on-book person, don't be concerned with the audience hearing your voice. The primary role of the on-book person is to support the reciter, and if you have ever been in the position of losing your train of thought or of having the deer-in-the-headlights experience, then you know how much of a relief it is to have someone get you back on track. In addition, since he or she is sitting in the front row and their voice is being projected forward toward the reciter and away from the audience. The audience frequently doesn't even realize that the reciter just received a prompt.

In preparation for what we hope will not happen, we _always_ do an exercise in rehearsal in which we "practice the mistake." Do not leave this as just a good idea, practice it. Have the reciter progress through the passage and then pretend to reach an impasse. The reciter should then look directly at the on-book person, and the on-book person should then call out the next few words. Make prompts from the on-book person a normal part of the rehearsal. Whether the reciter is pretending to forget or actually can't remember the next few words, it is important that the reciter knows that he or she has someone supporting him or her in this way.

Trust but Verify

The best friend of a teacher is the test, and the best test is the one for which the student is prepared. Just as the teacher is the ally of the student who is preparing for final examinations, the recitation leader is the ally of a reciter preparing for a recitation. Be a good ally and continually test your reciter. Put him or her in challenging situations (not embarrassing, just challenging!) and test his or her understanding, ability to think on his or her feet, and knowledge of the setting. The "start anywhere" exercise[7] is a good test, so are questions about the meaning of sections of the passage, "what if" questions that make the reciter think on their feet, and re-visiting choices of tone and tempo so the reciter recalls and defends why these choices were made. Each time the reciter passes a test, he or she becomes a little more confident, and you become an even better recitation leader.

---

[7] Details are in chapter 9 of this book in the "Memory Check" section

7

The Review Process

A diligent approach to recitation includes multiple reviews so that there is abundant opportunity to identify any areas that may misrepresent the intent of the passage. There are multiple levels of reviewing a recitation, and each has its purpose and strengths. The greater the variety of review, the greater the confidence of the reciter. The types of reviewers are:

- Family and friends
- Recitation leader
- Teacher or pastor

We will look at the contribution of each level of review and how this process not only provides the best path to an accurate presentation, but also fosters communication within the church family.

Family and Friends Review

Encourage the reciter to practice by reciting to their family or to a few close friends; people who will patiently listen to them and encourage them. It's a confidence boost and an opportunity to practice, but it also provides much more.

What would you think if a friend came to you with a notecard, on which he or she had written a Bible passage, and asked you to "spot him or her" as this person repeats it back to you? Would you make fun of your friend for not knowing it perfectly? Would you mock the delivery? Of course not! Most likely, you would help this person when he or she stumbled and would root for him or her. Not only that, but you also might learn something from the passage and even think about memorizing some of it yourself.

You will be encouraging your reciters to be role models for their children, their parents, their family, and maybe even for the guy standing behind them at the taqueria who was nice enough to follow along as they stumbled through John 3:12–15.

Recitation Leader Review

In the normal progression, during rehearsals the recitation leader will listen to the reciter and then provide some feedback. The feedback should serve multiple purposes. It should encourage the reciter to make progress and instill some confidence. The leader should also ensure that the tone and tempo of the presentation relates back to the meaning. Whereas friends and family listen to see if the reciter is getting the *words* right, the recitation leader is there to see if the *message* is right. He or she ensures that the reciter both knows the words of the passage and conveys the purpose of the writing. This review often makes memory recall easier because connections are being made between actions, words, tone, and feelings. The recitation leader should interject some memorization techniques[8] to bolster the reciter's memory of the passage.

---

[8] See chapter six of our companion book *The Art of Reciting Scripture*

Video or Self-Review

We typically record videos of all recitations and post them on our recitation website, https://ByHeart.org. It makes for a convenient way to share the event with people even if they are thousands of miles away—or would never cross the threshold of a church. A video link gives the reciter an opportunity to share his or her experience with distant family, neighbors, friends who couldn't be there, and even with colleagues. It's a personal way to "Go into all the world an preach the gospel to all creation" (Mark 16:15 NIV).

However, video isn't just for the final presentation; it can also provide keen feedback to the reciter during the preparation process. Video is an insightful observation that never lies. With video, the reciter can review his or her presentation and do his or her own critique. Encourage reciters to do this because they have a unique perspective. They were inside of the action, and now, on the outside, they can analyze whether it "feels the same on the inside as it looks on the outside." Their goal should be to find any incongruities in the message: tone, tempo, or motions for cases in which reciters thought they were conveying one thing, but realized that, from the outside, it looked like something else.

Teacher or Pastor Review

Getting a review from the person who will be presenting the teaching on the day that the recitation is planned to be presented is a wonderful opportunity for both parties. The teacher or pastor will also have studied the passage and will have a fresh outlook that will either reinforce what has been prepared so far, or else alert the team to a needed modification. This typically takes place just a few days before the recitation, so we're hoping that there are no big changes at this stage—but if there are, then be grateful that you are aware in enough time to make a change so that the passage is not misinterpreted.

8

Technical Setup

> "The Lord said to Moses, 'See, I have called by
> name Bezalel the son of Uri, son of Hur, of the tribe
> of Judah, and I have filled him with the Spirit of
> God, with ability and intelligence, with knowledge
> and all craftsmanship, to devise artistic designs, ...
> to work in every craft"
>
> —Exodus 31:1–5 (ESV)

The passage has been selected, and your reciter is ready. For weeks, you've been studying, preparing, and practicing. You know exactly what to do and have prepared your reciter to handle every situation. You are ready to have the Word spoken boldly.

Although having all of that is essential to a successful recitation, there are still more logistics that must be processed and accounted for before the big day. All too often, recitations run into problems with audio or visuals that can make even the best recitation seem disappointing.

With all the time and energy that you've put into selecting the passage, recruiting a reciter, coordinating schedules, and practicing, it would be a shame to let it go to waste by having an audio or other technical failure on the day of the recitation.

Although it seems incongruous that the pure, clear message of scripture would need help from the wired technology of the present age, the fact remains that to reach large groups, this is the case. I have heard the protests and felt the reluctance. Yes, plenty of reciters want to rely solely on their unamplified natural voices to be heard, and they confidently assert that their voices are powerful enough to fill every corner of the room.

Nonsense.

Mic up! Power on the projector, crank up the volume, and flip on the lights. The reciter needs to be heard and seen. I know that it is uncomfortable to hear one's amplified voice and to feel the heat of spotlights, but it is a small sacrifice that will allow your audience to experience the passage. This chapter will expose you to some possibilities for making use of the technology around us when delivering the pure and beautiful message of scripture.

Sound Setup

Let's start by talking about one of the most important pieces of AV technology you'll use on the day of the recitation: the microphone.

There are several types of microphones, and each has a purpose that matches its characteristics. Choosing the right microphone for the purpose can go a long way to ensuring that your reciters are heard loud and clear and that their message is delivered exactly the way it was envisioned. Let's dive into the types of microphones, their usage, and how to know which is right for you.

Here are the primary microphones used for recitations along with why they may be the right choice for you, including the pros and cons of using them.

Fixed-Position Microphone

Many churches have a microphone attached to the podium or on a mic stand in front of the podium. Ideally, these are adjustable for the height of the reciter, and the reciter adjusts the position of the mic to be in front of his or her mouth.

Pros	Cons
Hands-free	Stage movement is severely restricted
Excellent sound quality	Variations in mouth position affect the volume

Handheld Wireless Microphone

This type of microphone is one of the most common and is often seen at presentations, assemblies, and concerts. A wireless handheld microphone can be used by reciters to give them something to do with their hands which can help calm jittery nerves.

Pros	Cons
No cords to trip over	Depends heavily on good mic technique
Holding it may comfort nervous reciters	Constrains hand gestures

Headset Microphone

A wireless headset microphone is worn over the ear with the microphone on a thin wire near the reciter's mouth. A wire connects the microphone to a battery pack worn on the reciter's clothing.

Pros	Cons
Stable position, less chance of sound variation	Expensive
Hands-free	Need a place for the battery pack
No distraction to the reciter	

Lavalier Microphone

A lavalier microphone is also sometimes known as a *lav* or *lapel mic*. The *lapel* moniker suits its purpose nicely; it's essentially a discrete microphone worn on the lapel of a shirt or jacket and is used to allow the speaker to operate the microphone hands-free during the recitation. You can often see this type of microphone worn by TV newscasters on the evening news.

Pros	Cons
Stable position, less chance of sound variation	Need a place for the battery pack
Hands-free	Prone to picking up background noise
No distraction to the reciter	Mic needs to clip to something
	Brushing the mic will cause a loud noise

Microphone Technique

Handheld Microphone Technique

- Do not tap or blow into the microphone.
- Keep the mic at a fixed position relative to your face.
- Tilt the bottom of the mic down forty-five degrees so you don't block your face, and tilt with your wrist, not your arm.
- Place the mic two fingers' width from your mouth.
- The mic does not make you sound better.
- Practice with a microphone in your hand
- Always speak at full volume without depending on the mic to make up for deficiencies.

Headset Microphone Technique

- Situate the mic behind the corner of the reciter's mouth.
- Allow some slack in the cable at the back of the reciter's neck so that the reciter can twist his or her head to the right and left without binding the cable.
- Avoid placing the mic where fabric, hair, jewelry, or body parts may rub against it.
- Wear clothing that will accommodate placement of a wireless body pack and that will, in some way, conceal the wire that runs from the body pack to the headset.

Lavalier Microphone Technique

How and where the reciter wears the lavalier mic will either result in a nice clear sound or in irritating problems.

- Place the mic over the reciter's sternum to provide a nice balance of close-proximity and natural sound reproduction.
- Practice good cable management and ensure both the mic and cable look neat and tidy.
- Wear clothing that will accommodate placement of a wireless body pack and will conceal the wire running from the body pack to the headset.
- Avoid any gestures that may jolt the microphone

Your lavalier microphone will generally be supplied with a standard mic clip. This is the most popular option for securing a mic to your reciter, but it does require a physical edge of clothing to attach to, such as a jacket lapel or button-up shirt. This clip will be visible to the camera or audience, so it's important to make it as unobtrusive as possible.

Three techniques for achieving a clean, unobtrusive placement are: the broadcast loop; the hidden mic; and the vampire clip.

Broadcast Loop

For the broadcast loop[10], insert your mic into its clip; then loop the cable back up into it as well. When you attach the lavalier to your reciter's clothing, run the excess cable behind the fabric so all you see from the front is the microphone itself, the clip, and a small cable loop.

A broadcast loop.

Hidden Mic

To conceal your lav microphone[10] beneath clothing, it is common practice to use a tape technique to create a double-sided sticky pillow. Ensure you are using tape that will provide a strong hold and that will not move or come off during the recitation. Take a piece as long as your hand is wide and fold it into a triangle. Stick the microphone to it. Fold a second piece of tape into a triangle and stick it to the other side of the microphone. Place this double-sided sticky microphone pillow under the person's shirt, as high up as possible, to stay hidden. This technique helps to reduce sound of motion and even helps with wind if you are recording a video of a recitation outdoors.

A microphone pillow.

---

9 https://www.rode.com/blog/all/lavalier-mounting-best-practices.
10 https://www.youtube.com/watch?v=J7HXxo83Hs0.

Vampire Clips

A vampire is another simple, frequently used lavalier clip, perfect for when you have no edge of clothing to attach to. The vampire (or viper) clip will have two small pins, or teeth, that will secure it to a T-shirt, dress, or other fabric that a standard clip could not grip.

Lighting Setup

Because there is so much information conveyed through body language, the reciter must be seen. This is the realm of light and sightlines. Body language is not just an actor's domain; it is the common person's means of expression. The hands, the eyebrows, the tilt of the head, and the posture all convey meaning. Take away the ability to see the reciter, and you take away a portion of the meaning from the recitation.

Turn on the lights and raise the stage. It may be that you just need to turn the dimmers up. Spotlights (a.k.a. "follow spots") are the solution if your facility prefers to maintain a low-light setting.

If you are casting spotlights, then follow good practices:

- If you don't have sights on your follow spot, make some. Use copper wire (or a wire coat hanger) to fashion two small loops that you can attach to the top of the follow spot. Use black wrap tape to fix them if you have it; this won't melt when the lantern heats up.
- There are some manufacturers who make sights with added functions.[11]
- Use notes to indicate cues.
- Preadjust the beam width to the first cue.

---

[11] See http://www.theatrecrafts.com/pages/home/topics/lighting/followspotting-tips-tricks/.

Sightlines

With the lighting accommodated, the next concern is line of sight. If the floor is flat and level (no slope) then the seated audience has a problem. The head of one person can get in the way of the person who is sitting behind that head.

There are two choices: either raise the stage so that the sightline of the person sitting behind projects above the person in front's head, or rake (slope) the seats so that the person behind is sitting higher than the person in front. It is far easier to raise the stage.[12] "Ezra the teacher of the Law stood on a high wooden platform built for the occasion. … Ezra opened the book. All the people could see him because he was standing above them; and as he opened it, the people all stood up" (Nehemiah 8:4–5 NIV).

Take a tip from the early church and get your people up high enough to be seen. There was a reason for the elevated pulpit, and it wasn't to make the preacher seem closer to God; it was to provide a visual answer to the question, "Who is speaking?"

Pulpit at Wootton Wawen Warwickshire.

---

[12] The terms *downstage*, referring to the front of the stage, and *upstage*, referring to the back of the stage, come from venues that sloped the stage with the back of the stage higher than the front.

And yet, perfectly rational people resist raising the stage, citing reasons of humility and awkwardness. I don't buy that. If your intent is to convey a message, and if your goal is to influence people, then you need to get your body where it can be seen. The trouble is less about humility and more about fear, because when you are on an elevated stage, then you are exposed. One must love the audience enough that the fear of being on a stage is overcome by one's love for the people who are being addressed. "There is no fear in love. But perfect love drives out fear" (1 John 4:18a NIV).

When you build the stage, make it high enough, strong enough, and quiet enough to do its job. A squeaky, wobbly stage is not only distracting, but also unsafe.

One more stage comment: when possible, include a crawl space under the stage so that electrical and sound cabling can be rerouted. This helps reduce the clutter of cabling onstage, which can be a tripping hazard. If a crawl space is not feasible, then tape the cables down. The effort is worth it if it prevents someone from tripping on a cable and getting injured.

Projection Setup

The quality of the projected image that forms the backdrop of the recitation depends on the setup of the projection system. Churches have come a long way from the days of overhead projectors and grease pencils. Although a good recitation does not depend on a projected image, if you choose to use one, you will want to ensure that the image serves its purpose.

1. The Right Projector in the Right Location

Where you mount your projector depends, at least partly, on the projector that you have. And the projector that you get will depend on where you plan on mounting it. You'll need enough space for the projection itself to be seen by the entire audience. The bigger, the better.

Brightness

A key factor to consider when buying a church projector is its brightness. The brightness rating determines how bright projected images are. Ambient lighting works in opposition. Most churches have a moderate- to medium amount of ambient lighting coming through the windows that can wash out projected images, thus affecting the visibility.

Because projectors in churches are often used to display text, they need a higher brightness rating. Text will appear more clearly when projectors have a high brightness rating. A church projector should have a brightness rating of at least 4,000 ANSI lumens. Churches with a large seating capacity can consider projectors with 5,000 or even 6,000 ANSI lumens rating. Churches or houses of worship wherein the ambient lighting can be controlled using window blinds or other means can opt for a 2,500 to 3,000 ANSI lumens projector.

Resolution

Another factor to consider when choosing a church projector is its resolution. A projector's resolution impacts the detail level of the projected images. The right resolution for a church projector will depend on the type of content it will project. A church or house of worship that will primarily use a projector for presentations or for showing text can consider a projector with a resolution of 1024×768 (XGA) pixels. XGA projectors are ideal for displaying large text and are quite cheap. If you are projecting movies and videos in widescreen formats, then consider a projector with an HD (1920×1080 pixels) resolution.

Distance from the Projector Screen: Throw Ratio

When installed at a specific distance from the screen, the throw ratio of a projector determines the size of the projected image. Projectors can be classified into three different categories based on their throw ratios:

- **Ultra-short throw** projects (ratio of 0.4 or less) are meant to be installed close to the screen. They can project large images at just a few inches away from a screen.
- **Short-throw** ratio projectors (0.4 to 1.0) are designed to be installed a few feet from the screen.
- **Standard throw** projectors have a ratio greater than 1.0 and are installed several feet away from the screen. These projectors produce large images when they are placed far away.

An ultra-short throw projector may project a ninety-six-inch image at a distance of six inches from the screen. However, when a standard throw projector is placed at the six inch distance, the image projected by it may have a size of around twelve inches on an average. Therefore, it is important to consider the distance that the projector will be installed from the screen.

To get bigger images, you need to move the projector farther back. And, unless you mount the projector on the ceiling, you won't be able to have people sitting in the path of the beam. Consider the seating arrangement when deciding where the projector should be. If the projector is mounted to the ceiling, be sure that the area near the intake fan is kept clean and not in direct line of air or heat vents.

2. Set Up the Screen

A screen provides a uniform blank surface that can reflect or even amplify your projector's light better than a wall and also delivers a brighter image. You should select a screen material that's well-suited to your projector and room. The gain of the screen material is an important aspect in choosing a screen. *Gain* is a measure of the reflectivity of a screen (i.e., the amount of light that a projector reflects to the viewers).

Different screen coatings applied to the base vinyl screen material are used to achieve different gain values. High-gain screens reflect more light, which can help provide a brighter, less washed-out image in bright rooms or with lower-lumen projectors. One downside to higher-gain screens is that they can suffer from "hot-spotting," where part of the screen looks noticeably brighter. This is because they reflect the light back in a narrower, more focused band. The picture will look best to viewers who sit directly in front of the screen rather than off to the sides.

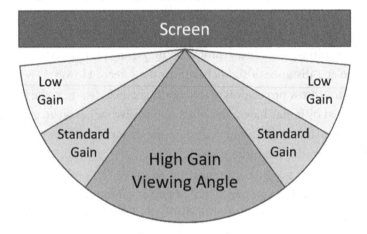

As screen gain increases, the optimum viewing angle decreases.

If you have a wide seating area, you might want to consider a screen with standard gain because it will reflect the light evenly in all directions. This is also called neutral gain, or it may be listed numerically as a gain of 1.0.

Screens with negative gain also offer wide viewing angles. They were designed to deliver deeper blacks by absorbing some of the projector's light. Since they reduce all the reflected light (not just the projector's light), they can also help mitigate issues with ambient light in the room. These screens are often used with high-lumen projectors to compensate for the amount of light they absorb.

3. Get the Right Height

Most projectors are designed to line up roughly with the middle of the lens a bit above the bottom edge of the screen. However, doing so means that the noise of the projector is at ear level and that the path of the beam forces the seating arrangement to accommodate it. More frequently, you will mount the projector up high and then adjust the image keystone that will result. Be sure to get a projector that has keystone correction. The trade-off with keystone correction is that it impairs resolution a bit.

4. Project an Alignment Image

To get the projected image looking its best, you'll want to have a reference test pattern. Some projectors have built-in test patterns for this purpose, but if yours doesn't, you could use a setup disc or download an image online.

5. Adjust the Projected Image

Line up the center of the lens with the center of the screen. Make sure the projector is as level and perpendicular as possible, relative to the screen. The far edges of the projected image should be the same size, and ideally, the entire screen should be filled. If it's available, you can use the zoom control to size the image properly.

Adjust focus until details are sharp. Walk closer to the screen to check, if you can't tell. If the center is in focus but the corners aren't, it could be an indication that the projector and screen aren't quite perpendicular.

To fine-tune, you can use the adjustable legs and supports on the projector. If you create too much of an angle, you can use the keystone control to correct it.

6. Select the Right Picture Mode

Like TVs, projectors have preset picture modes, so you'll want to choose the right one. The best one for overall picture quality in a dark room is typically "movie" or "cinema." If you're dealing with ambient light, you might want to choose a brighter mode, but be aware that these often skew green.

9

The Day of the Recitation

When the day of the recitation arrives, it is important for the reciter to stay focused on the message and not be distracted. This can only happen if the recitation leader paves the way, ensuring that every detail has been managed. There are checks that need to be completed, people with whom to coordinate, and a nervous reciter needing guidance.

Throughout this preparation, be the calm, reasonable voice. Tell him or her what to expect. Encourage them. This is not the time to bring up anything new. If it hasn't been practiced in the weeks leading up to the recitation, do not introduce it now.

The reciter should show up forty-five to sixty minutes before the service begins. The leader should arrive an additional thirty minutes before that to get ahead of the preparation items.

Checklist

On the day of the recitation, ensure that you have completed the following:

✓ An order of worship and transitions have been defined, and all involved people have been notified.

✓ Arrangements have been made to move any onstage obstacles for the reciter.

✓ The person on-book has a copy of the text.

✓ A microphone has been positioned (especially the headset), and an onstage sound check has been completed.

✓ The reciter knows how to turn on and off the microphone.

✓ The reciter has arrived early and warmed up their voice.

✓ The reciter has performed a dry run of the passage.

✓ Graphics have been provided to the projection team.

✓ The projection team has been briefed on when graphics should be displayed.

✓ A video recorder is in place (optional).

Regarding the order of worship, we have learned through experience that if the reciter has another obligation just before the recitation, he or she will be more prone to problems during the recitation. It takes time to switch gears from one task to another and switching to "recitation mode" requires both focused effort and time. It is unfair to the reciter to burden him or her with any other duties just before the recitation. If the reciter sings on the worship team, this is a good week to get a replacement for him or her. This also applies if he or she collects the offering, teaches Sunday school, serves on the tech team, greets people, or makes coffee. The reciter needs to settle down and focus just before the recitation. As the leader, you make sure that he or she has that opportunity.

Let's take a closer look at three of these items: the sound check, the memory check, and the confirmation of cues.

The Sound Check

The sound check can be one of the most disconcerting moments on the day of recitation. People are milling about, musicians are tuning their instruments, lights are being adjusted, and it is, generally, a random atmosphere. Meanwhile, the reciter is recalling the passage, not knowing where to look or whether anyone is listening to him or her. The unnatural experience of hearing his or her own voice over the sound system while the sound is being adjusted can be disconcerting.

Prepare the reciter for the sound check so that he or she does not get shaken by the experience. Expect that it will be chaotic and seek to focus the reciter on the mechanics of getting onstage, identifying where the on-book person will be seated, and on the beauty of the passage.

Do at least one check with the on-book person prompting the reciter. Even though you will have practiced it before, things sound different when using a microphone. This is also necessary so that the reciter knows where the on-book person will be sitting. The key to prompting is knowing where to look for the prompt.

If there is a lavalier microphone with a battery pack, and it is powered off until just before the recitation, then the reciter will need to know how to turn it on and off and will need to be cued as to when to turn it on. Sometimes the battery pack is mounted in a position that is difficult for the reciter to access. In this case, someone who knows how to turn the pack on, how to confirm that it is on, and who can quietly accomplish this needs to help.

The Memory Check

The reciter will certainly want to run through the passage before the recitation, and this is typically also just before the sound check. Let the reciter run through it a couple of times to gain confidence. Then lead him or her through two exercises that are most important when preparing for the stage.

When there is a hiccup in a recitation, you don't get to go back and start over. You must be able to recognize phrases and to pick up in the middle. The "start anywhere" exercise prepares the reciter for this scenario. It goes like this: You read a short phrase from the passage, and the reciter then continues from that point for a short time. Then find another point in the passage, read a short phrase, and then the reciter should continue from that point. The selections should be random. The only thing to watch for is if a phrase occurs the same way in more than one place in the passage. The reciter must be given enough information to distinguish which part of the passage is the source of his or her prompt.

This is an excellent way to get the reciter's head in the game. It is also an important confidence builder. Plowing through from start to finish with no breaks is helpful, but the ability to start anywhere is where you really want to invest your time.

This run-through is also a good time to rehearse with the on-book person. Tell the reciter to start reciting the passage and then, at some point, pretend to be unable to continue. The on-book person sits in the middle of the first row, and the rhythm[13] is like this:

1. Reciter stops speaking.
2. The on-book person looks up.
3. If it is just a natural pause, the on-book person does nothing.
4. If the reciter is struggling, then he or she will look directly at the on-book person. The on-book person then speaks the next two or three words loudly. Do not whisper or mouth the words. Be loud. Remember, the on-book person is seated at the front, and his or her voice is directed toward the stage. The rest of the audience will hardly be aware.

Confirming Cues

The worst thing for a recitation is being surprised. Whether the reciter is surprised by a sound in the middle of the recitation, a light that suddenly begins to flash, or an object on the stage that gets in

---

[13] Also described in the "On-Book Person" section in chapter 6 of this book

the way, all surprises can jar the reciter. One of the worst surprises occurs when there is uncertainty about when the recitation will occur, and then reciter is abruptly called up to recite. Not knowing cues puts the reciter on edge and adds an unnecessary strain.

To avoid this, make sure that you get a listing of the order of events. This will ensure that the reciter knows when he or she will be going onstage. Talk to the person or people who are scheduled immediately before the reciter (i.e., "the predecessor") and discuss the transition. Include in this discussion:

- How long the predecessor will be onstage before calling up the reciter.
- What the predecessor will be saying in conclusion (i.e., the cue for the reciter).
- Whether a microphone handoff is needed. If so, from whom?
- Establish the walking paths for the transition.

If this information is not already written down, then write it on a piece of paper. In the minutes leading up to the recitation, you and the reciter will both be glad that the order is written down. Uncertainties seem to grow in those minutes and being able to refer to some hard evidence is calming. Knowing this information means that you can cue the reciter as the time approaches, and you can also keep a look out for any surprises regarding obstacles onstage.

For the reciter, there should be absolutely no instructions about what to do after the recitation. Avoid asking the reciter to move any objects, make an announcement after the recitation, or help with anything else. If these things are needed and there is no one else to do them, then the recitation leader should do the task him- or herself. The reciter can't be put into a spot where he or she must remember to do anything other than what has been practiced and perfected. The leader will need to absorb any "extras" that get thrown toward the reciter.

Warm-Ups for Reciters

Singers are not the only people who need to warm up before going onstage, reciters do as well. Warm-ups serve several purposes, not the least of which is to relax and focus the reciter. The activities and exercises you lead will help to settle them. You will have done your job if you can get the reciter past their jitters and tension to the point of longing to speak the message.

By the day of the recitation, the reciters will already have spent hours in preparation, studying the passage to understand its intent, memorizing the words, and developing a natural pattern for delivery. The day of the recitation, however, is a journey in itself and the reciter will need someone to talk them through the events of the day and ensure that they are both physically and mentally limber.

The following "articulator exercises" [14,15,16] are intended to address the physical portion of the warm-up and they do a good job of preparing the physical person. At the same time, in your role as leader, you should also remind the reciters about the purpose of the recitation. Keep them grounded and aware of the sequence of events that they should expect. Help the reciters to visualize each step so they are prepared mentally as you also use some exercises from each of the three groups described below to prepare them physically:

Awaken Sleeping Parts

1. Lips
   a. Blow through your lips to flutter them
   b. Stretch the corners of your mouth – wide, then narrow
   c. Open your mouth wide, scrunch your mouth closed

---

[14] Howcast.com https://www.youtube.com/watch?v=O86VWsXt-M4
[15] Verba https://www.youtube.com/watch?v=hb1Cv7aDXmk
[16] Stage Milk https://www.youtube.com/watch?v=8sQoYa8TptI

2. Tongue
   a. Blow through your tongue to flutter the tongue
   b. Stick out your tongue and widen it, then narrow it (difficult!)

3. Face
   a. Shake out your face

4. Soft Palate
   a. Yawn full face
   b. Yawn on one side, then the other

5. Diaphragm
   a. Make ten sharp, short "ch" sounds. Put your hand just below your rib cage and feel the sharp contractions. This is your diaphragm and it has a crucial role in speech.

Loosen muscles

1. Loosen the Tongue
   a. Touch every tooth, front and back
   b. Draw circles inside your cheek with the tip of your tongue
   c. Place the tip of your tongue behind the back of the bottom front teeth and keep it there as you force your tongue forward and back

2. Loosen key muscles
   a. Neck (gently!)
      i. Look down, look up, look left, look right
      ii. Head rolls to loosen the neck

b. Jaw

    i. Massage the jaw muscle (masseter) in circles and strokes

c. Cheeks (gently!)

    i. Pinch and knead like dough

d. Lips

    i. Pinch and pull your lips in all directions (with clean hands)

Create Sounds

1. Articulate around your tongue

    a. Stick out your tongue and then recite the passage with your tongue stuck out.

    b. A variation of this is to put a pencil in your clenched teeth and then recite your passage with the pencil held between your teeth

2. Voiced and un-voiced patterns.

    a. A voiceless sound is one that just uses air to make the sound and not the voice. You can tell whether a sound is voiced by putting your hand gently on your throat. When you say a sound, if you can feel a vibration it is a voiced sound.

    b. Un-voiced patterns: Pa, Ta, Ka. Speak this pattern quickly:

    > pa-ta-ka-pa-ta-ka-pa-ta-ka-Pah
    > pa-ta-ka-pa-ta-ka-pa-ta-ka-Pee
    > pa-ta-ka-pa-ta-ka-pa-ta-ka-Paw
    > pa-ta-ka-pa-ta-ka-pa-ta-ka-Poo
    > pa-ta-ka-pa-ta-ka-pa-ta-ka-Pay

    c. Voiced patterns: Ba, Da, Ga quickly:

    > ba-da-ga-ba-da-ga-ba-da-ga-Bah
    > ba-da-ga-ba-da-ga-ba-da-ga-Baw

ba-da-ga-ba-da-ga-ba-da-ga-Boo
ba-da-ga-ba-da-ga-ba-da-ga-Bee
ba-da-ga-ba-da-ga-ba-da-ga-Bay

3. Tongue twisters. Work on both speed and accuracy.
    a. Unique New York, New York unique
    b. Red leather, yellow leather
    c. She says she shall sew a sheet
    d. A big, black bug bit a big black bear and the big black bear bled blue black blood
    e. Peter Piper picked a peck of pickled peppers, a peck of pickled peppers Peter Piper picked
    f. Lesser leather never weathered lesser wetter weather

Visuals

We are visual creatures, therefore some attention needs to be given to what the audience will see. It becomes part of the message being communicated. The clothing, backdrop and surroundings can either serve to complement the message, or they can be distractions.

The clothing of the reciter needs to be functional as well as decorative. It must accommodate technical equipment. The reciter will need to plan for where the battery pack will be stowed, where the microphone will be clipped, and where the cables will be routed so as not to distract the audience. This consideration will also include hair and jewelry. Not all hairstyles work well with microphones, and jewelry rubbing against a microphone makes a disturbing noise. Besides the functional aspect, keep the following in mind when discussing clothing with your reciter:

- The clothing should be comfortable. Let's not add to the challenges that face the reciter. Clothing should not constrict motion and should feel good to wear.

- The clothing should align with the passage. This doesn't mean period-costumes or apparel, but it does mean that there shouldn't be a contradiction between the clothes being worn and the message being delivered.
- The clothing shouldn't draw attention. This would detract from the message.

During a recitation, you may also provide a graphic or PowerPoint slide that shows the reference for the passage and serves as a backdrop. For our reciters, we like to incorporate meaningful art in the backdrop. The slide also helps to remind the audience about where the passage being recited can be found. The slide backdrop can also serve as a reference after the recitation, when reviewing pictures and videos, so that it is clear which passage was being recited.

Art reinforces the recitation.

The art is meant to reinforce and deepen the message being presented. Each passage has multiple dimensions: the meaning of the words themselves, the context in which they are presented, and the tone and rhythm of the message. Visual images extend the dimensionality of the passage to the visual. I strongly advise against projecting the words of the passage while the reciter is speaking. It is too distracting for everyone.

In addition to the reference slide, we like to communicate something about the reciter: his or her name, family, and vocation.

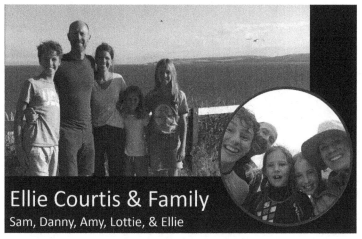

Example of a family slide.

This is one way that we grow in fellowship. We display a family picture and have the reciter introduce him- or herself. The goals of this are:

- **To make connections between people**. Someone may know a father but not realize who his children are, or they may know a mother but not know who her husband is. It's not just about the reciter. Seeing the picture helps with making these connections, especially for newcomers.

- **To provide the family context** in which God's Word is being expressed in life. If I see someone reciting a passage on perseverance, and I see that he or she has lots of kids, it may make a bridge that connects me to the reciter or to someone in the reciter's family.

- **To connect common interests or a profession** that the listening audience may share with the reciter.

10

Enhance the Recitation

Recitations take only a little time. Even a "long" recitation, such as reciting an entire chapter, takes only five to seven minutes. More commonly, the recitation takes one to two minutes. Like cooking a fine meal, the hours of preparation for a recitation result in a few minutes to savor the results. If, in addition to the recitation, the reciter would like to share from his or her experience with the passage, then here are three formats that accommodate commentary and can enhance the recitation.

Context Comments

Reciters may have a few words about their recitation passages that they would like to share before the recitation itself. This may allow them to set the context by summarizing the section that precedes their passage, or it may be a time to share the connections they have with the passage itself.

If your reciter is planning to include context comments before his or her recitation, then spend some time developing these comments together. The reciter needs to determine the *exact wording* of the comments he or she would like to share. Have the reciter practice making the comments and then transitioning to reciting. Don't leave this to chance; practice it as fully and as seriously as the rest of the recitation. The comments should provide information needed to understand the passage or understand the personal significance of the passage. Well-thought-out comments will also connect to the larger picture of the day's teaching. This means that it is a good idea to get the pastor or teacher involved to ensure the reciter's comments will be welcome and helpful.

Short Interview

After the recitation is complete, there is another opportunity for the reciter to share something regarding their recitation. In a short interview, the pastor/teacher asks one or two leading questions to prompt the reciter. This gives the reciter an opportunity to give some observation from his or her experience, potentially either this person's unique perspective on the passage or something about his or her experience with the process of preparing to recite. As with every part of the recitation, preparation and knowing what information is to be shared is the key to a clear message. The reciter should meet with the person asking the question(s) beforehand to discuss these and any response(s).

In-depth Interview

Our pastor has the humility to understand that he is not the sole source of teaching. Occasionally, we do a full interview in which the reciter can speak in depth about their passage. This occurs after the recitation and stands in the place of a sermon. The interview is structured and developed over a series of meetings between the reciter and the pastor.

Pastor interviewing a reciter.

Instead of hearing just one voice from the pulpit, you have two or more people speaking about the passage and interacting with each other. It is a lively format and provides variety to the order of worship.

When preparing for the interview, consider questions that bring out the reciter's unique insight into the passage. These need not be deep theological questions, but rather, questions about the tone and rhythm of the passage. A reciter is intimately connected with the wording and pattern of the passage and may have developed an emotional connection to the passage. Spending so much time with the passage, the reciter will also have some experience with how his or her understanding of it evolved over the course of preparation.

Here are some example questions that you may want to include in the interview:

1. How did you decide to recite this passage?
2. As you were memorizing and meditating on these verses, what did you notice about the tone of the passage? Was there any point where you felt that the tone shifted?

3. Were there portions of the passage that were difficult for you to decide how to voice?

4. What was your favorite portion of the passage?

5. Were there any sections of the passage that you didn't initially understand, or for which your understanding changed as you spent time with the passage?

6. What were some of the things the Lord taught you as you memorized this passage?

7. How did this passage affect your relationship with God and with those around you?

If the reciter and pastor have a good rapport and there are portions of the passage that are open to discussion, it can be a very engaging exchange. Hearing two people knowledgably discussing a biblical passage and presenting different perspectives can engage the audience.

11

After the Recitation

All the preparation for the recitation has paid off. The recitation has gone well. Hopefully, hearts have been moved, and the message for which the passage was written has been conveyed with accuracy and integrity. That is a good reason to celebrate. But what now?

There are several options for what happens after the recitation that will use all the experience gained so far and expand their scope. Some are internal to the church, such as an open mic night or delivering the recitation to the Sunday school classes. Others are external, reaching out into the community for other venues.

Another post-recitation activity is to get the release forms signed. When there are pictures or videos involved, then you must be clear about your intent and get permission from both the reciter and the photographer that publishing these is OK with them.

This chapter is meant to cover all of the post-recitation activities.

Do it Again!

If your reciter has delivered a passage to a congregation at *your* church, then encourage him or her to multiply the blessing. This person may need your encouragement and coordination skills, but it will be worth it. Connect with the people who lead home groups, women's ministries, men's ministries, and youth groups. There may even be leaders of other churches who would enjoy having a fresh face speaking the Word accurately.

On this last point, don't be too discouraged if the pastors that you approach do not respond immediately with open arms and welcoming hugs. Church leaders need to be wary and they are called to protect their flock from heresy, so an outsider must be scrutinized.

Recite at an Open Mic Night

An open mic night is an invitation to everyone who has memorized a passage, or to anyone who would like to hear scripture spoken, to come together and freely share. Maybe someone is preparing to recite and would like to get the feel for presenting to an audience, or someone has recited previously and would just like to keep sharp, or someone just wants to share a passage. Whoever it may be, everyone joins together—preferably in a room with a stage—and the mic is open, even if there is no mic at all. It's first come, first served. When a reciter finishes, he or she has the option of requesting feedback or of just letting the next person take the stage.

You will thoroughly enjoy an open mic night. It is as pure as the Word itself. Organize and advertise it with specific start and end times; about an hour is good, but just know that it will end too soon.

Create a Testimonial

The mission of By Heart Ministries is to connect people with the message of the Bible. The testimonies of people who have joined this mission will reflect the mission itself. The testimonies may be long or short and can have many elements, but they should all have these three components: the people, the passage, and the connection.

Here is an excellent example:

> "Committing my baptismal passage (Titus 3:3–7)
> to memory has been a beautiful experience. It's like
> a gift that keeps on giving because it's always there
> in my mind as a reminder of how God brought me
> out of the darkness into the light."
>
> —Steve Gibbons

Steve's connection to the passage can touch each person who understands his testimony. It's a beautiful passage that contains both salvation and the trinity, so when you layer in the thought that this passage helped someone—this specific person—out of the darkness, then you will have a new connection as well. The next time you read Titus 3:3–7, think about how important and meaningful the passage is to Steve.

Beyond the people, passage, and connection, the testimony may have a component in which the reciter describes what the process was like for him or her, including how the process of preparing for a recitation affected his or her faith walk and relationships. This is important information for others who are considering reciting. You, as the person shepherding the recitation, can encourage the reciter to develop his or her recitation story. The reciter's testimony can spark people to investigate the claims of the Bible as well as to fuel the faith of the faithful.

> "Preparing for my recitation helped me to picture
> the events quite vividly, like the cliché 'it made
> it come alive'—but that's true! A great learning
> experience!"
>
> —Kerry Wheatcroft

Post the Video

Make a video of the recitation available for others to enjoy it again or to see what they missed. Videos can be both inspirational and instructional.

We post ours to a video-sharing website and then link to the videos from our church's web pages. This allows the link to be shared directly and accessed via our web portal.

Legalities

Publication Agreement

We video every recitation and often take pictures. Depending on your home country, there may be privacy laws that prohibit publicly sharing images of a person unless that person specifically grants you the right. Where I live, in Germany, that is certainly the case. I think that it is very civilized and appropriate to give the person the right of refusal. If someone does not want his or her image either published or posted, then it should not be. There should be no further discussion.

It is your obligation to submit a request that allows you to publish the image of anybody represented in your pictures or videos. Everybody—even your best friends or family members—needs to provide you with permission. There is no such thing as an "assumed permission." Get it in writing.

A simple email or note will be enough to make it clear that the reciter will allow his or her image to be published in the public domain. This should be formalized in a document that establishes the rights granted by the person. The document should include the person's promise not to sue for legal claims such as libel or invasion of privacy.

One aspect that you may need to struggle with is regarding the scope of the request. If someone reads the fine print of an image release that states: "the right to use my image for all purposes, including advertising, trade, or any commercial purpose throughout the world and in perpetuity," they may suddenly become a little bit less agreeable. The words *for all purposes* and *in perpetuity* seem a little extreme. I know that the release is meant to protect the photographer and publisher, but it also seems to give them license to be reckless. My preference causes more work for me but makes everyone else more comfortable. My approach is to request a release for a specific purpose or purposes. For example, to "use the image on the ByHeart. org website" or to "use in promotional videos and posters for the International Christian Fellowship Church." Those are still broad in scope, but they won't make it okay to use the images in monster truck show posters or in videos to sell unhealthy foods.

The exact contents of the agreement are between you and the subject but be sure to get an agreement. If you don't, there are legal consequences that can cost you real money. Be sure to find an agreement form that suits you and use it consistently.

See Appendix II for some example documents.

12

Recitation Art

The core of the message that is conveyed in a recitation begins with the heart of God and what he is communicating to us. What we see are the words. To these words, we add our tone and tempo, body language, movement, and pacing to give layers of depth. Another layer that can deepen the message is art—something that comes in through your eyes and evokes an emotion.

Art can work synergistically with the presentation of scripture in making an emotional connection beyond the words. The use of emoticons or emojis to pictorially convey a message is a more banal way of doing the same thing. Images convey a lot of information, and when there is an image that reinforces a passage of scripture, then we can connect the two and deepen the impact of the message.

All the layers—the words, the movement, the energy, the pacing, and the art—when put together, should bring us back to the origin of the message, the heart of God communicating to his loved ones.

Art that Works with Recitations

Not all art works in conjunction with a recitation. There is amazing art that, however good, would serve only as a distraction. The best situation is when the work of art has a strong central message that makes an impression. *Reconciliation*, a sculpture by Josefina de Vasconcellos, is such a work. Although there is a flood of nuance and personal depth that we bring to viewing this work, the message is clear and powerful. The two people in this sculpture seem to have dropped an enormous burden and their arms are relaxed yet clinging to one another—not trying to contain or constrain, but to bond. It feels like there is sorrow as their heads are buried in each other's shoulders as if to hide the tears.

It's not that a work of art can't be complex, but it should not require concentration that takes the viewer's attention away from the other layers of the message. It's a balance.

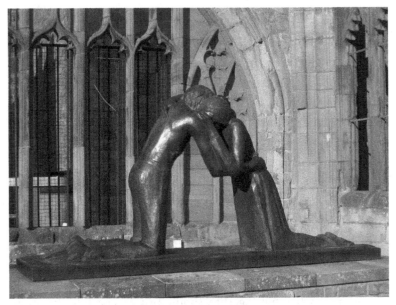

Pastor interviewing a reciter.

Artist: **Josefina de Vasconcellos, 1977**
Title: ***Reconciliation***
Passage: Genesis 50:15–21 (NIV). Joseph Reassures His Brothers

> When Joseph's brothers saw that their father was
> dead, they said, "What if Joseph holds a grudge

against us and pays us back for all the wrongs we did to him?" So they sent word to Joseph, saying, "Your father left these instructions before he died: 'This is what you are to say to Joseph: I ask you to forgive your brothers the sins and the wrongs they committed in treating you so badly.' Now please forgive the sins of the servants of the God of your father." When their message came to him, Joseph wept. His brothers then came and threw themselves down before him. "We are your slaves," they said. But Joseph said to them, "Don't be afraid. Am I in the place of God? You intended to harm me, but God intended it for good to accomplish what is now being done, the saving of many lives. So then, don't be afraid. I will provide for you and your children." And he reassured them and spoke kindly to them.

Genesis 50:15–21 (NIV)

Connecting Recitation with Art

When selecting a work of art to accompany a recitation, the connection between the art and the passage can either be made by you, or by the artist. I'd like to give an example of both possibilities.

Artist Makes the Art Connection

I sent a request to an artist, David Woodford, asking if he had a work of art that could accompany John 3:1–15 (the story of Nicodemus with Jesus). David replied that he had one that really fit the bill. It was entitled *Six Degrees of Separation*, and his concept was that it "expresses the academic conundrums that Nicodemus presented to

Jesus … I can imagine him trying to get his head around all the angles but Jesus cuts through all of the intellectual arguments and gets to the heart of the matter. Jesus' comments on the darkness and light might well be supported by the print as well" (David Woodford).

He sent me the piece and, after viewing it, I saw why David had selected it. I saw the sharp edges that David had mentioned, and I saw the red dot in each of the six views as being what seemed to Nicodemus to be a moving target. He kept thinking he had the target in scope, and then Jesus's answers made him question whether they were even talking about the same thing! The sharp edges of dogmatic teaching were being frustrated by this target that refused to stay put.

Six degrees of separation, a collagraph by David Woodford

Passage: John 3:1–15 (NIV)

There was a man named Nicodemus, a Jewish religious leader who was a Pharisee. After dark one evening, he came to speak with Jesus. "Rabbi," he said, "we all know that God has sent you to teach us. Your miraculous signs are evidence that God is with you." Jesus replied, "I tell you the truth, unless you are born again, you cannot see the Kingdom of God."

"What do you mean?" exclaimed Nicodemus. "How can an old man go back into his mother's womb and be born again?"

Jesus replied, "I assure you, no one can enter the Kingdom of God without being born of water and the Spirit. Humans can reproduce only human life, but the Holy Spirit gives birth to spiritual life. So don't be surprised when I say, 'You must be born again.' The wind blows wherever it wants. Just as you can hear the wind but can't tell where it comes from or where it is going, so you can't explain how people are born of the Spirit."

"How are these things possible?" Nicodemus asked. Jesus replied, "You are a respected Jewish teacher, and yet you don't understand these things? I assure you, we tell you what we know and have seen, and yet you won't believe our testimony. But if you don't believe me when I tell you about earthly things, how can you possibly believe if I tell you about heavenly things? No one has ever gone to heaven and returned. But the Son of Man has come down from heaven. And as Moses lifted up the bronze snake on a pole in the wilderness, so the Son of Man must be lifted up, so that everyone who believes in him will have eternal life.

John 3:1–15 (NIV)

Leader or Reciter makes an Art Connection

The connection is not always as easy as simply asking an artist for an appropriate piece of art and them providing the perfect one. Sometimes it takes some searching, and that can be fun. When you do, have some concepts in mind that embody the passage so you can search with intentionality. There needs to be a discipline even in the search for art because it becomes another layer of the message and must be congruous with the rest of the message.

For a recitation of Isaiah 9:2–7, by Peter S., we were looking for a piece of art that would accompany the passage. Here are the concepts used to guide the search:

- Overcoming oppression,
- Darkness being overcome by light, and
- Justice triumphing.

We found a piece by Danielle Harth. It was titled *2 Samuel 22: The Rescue of David*. It is a powerful painting, and I was not put off by the title not matching the passage of the recitation. I loved how, in this painting, it felt like justice was triumphing, overcoming the fire and flood. Both fire and flood can seem so unfair when people lose everything, including loved ones. Our hearts break to hear about a fire that destroyed someone's house and every vestige of memory in it. We are devastated by water and mudslides that bury homes that were full of life. It can seem arbitrarily cruel when families suffer these loses. This painting shows both forces in their full fury, and yet there seems to be a third element that overcomes them both.

2 Samuel 22: The Rescue of David, by Danielle
Harth (www.danielleharth.com)

Passage: Isaiah 9:2–7 (NLT)

The people who walk in darkness will see a great
light. For those who live in a land of deep darkness,
a light will shine. You will enlarge the nation of
Israel, and its people will rejoice. They will rejoice
before you as people rejoice at the harvest and like
warriors dividing the plunder. For you will break
the yoke of their slavery and lift the heavy burden
from their shoulders. You will break the oppressor's
rod, just as you did when you destroyed the army of
Midian. The boots of the warrior and the uniforms
bloodstained by war will all be burned. They will
be fuel for the fire.

For a child is born to us, a son is given to us.
The government will rest on his shoulders. And he
will be called: Wonderful Counselor, Mighty God,

Everlasting Father, Prince of Peace. His government and its peace will never end.

He will rule with fairness and justice from the throne of his ancestor David for all eternity. The passionate commitment of the Lord of Heaven's Armies will make this happen!

Isaiah 9:2–7 (NLT)

Artist Relationships

Art can serve as the visual link to a biblical passage. It can embody the emotion, energy, and even the ambiguity of the spoken word for our eyes. It can be a valuable component of a recitation, whether the recitation is performed live or recorded on video.

Therefore, it is only fair that we get permission to use an artist's work if it is being presented during a recitation or in a recitation video. You need to contact the artist and request his or her permission. My experience is that artists are generally happy to have their art shared and feel respected because you are asking their permission. However, this is not always the case. There are artists that want nothing to do with a Christian message. That's fine. Respect their wishes.

In reaching out to artists, you are creating a new relationship and exposing them to the good work you are doing. That's a win, no matter what the response. Here is an example of an email that you may send to an artist:

I'm writing to request your permission to use a picture of your painting, named *Cosmic Seed* in a presentation of a memorized passage from the Bible. The passage that will be recited is Titus 3:3-7. Our goal in reciting is to speak the words of the Bible clearly to convey the meaning of the passage just as clearly and naturally as two friends speaking to one another.

We have found that art helps by visually representing what the words are saying and thereby deepening the impact of the message.

I hope that you will give me permission to use your art for this purpose. If so, please respond with this message by indicating, "I give you permission to use *Cosmic Seed* in your recitation."

Be sure to follow up after the recitation with a note to the artist and a picture from the recitation or a link to the video. You never know what lives can be changed by this simple point of connection.

Acknowledgments

With heartfelt gratitude, I'd like to thank the following for their contributions and inspiration in supporting and encouraging me in creating this book. To Carol Griffin for being my sounding board; to Naomi Woodford for her precise editing and acumen; to Darren Ho, who mentored me in discipleship; to Carsten Lotz, whose unbridled enthusiasm lifts me; to Gary Darnell, whose keen insight and love of the Word kept me on an even keel; to Dan Register and Jim Jahncke for their contributions to the technical chapters; to Tom Asai for his steadfast loyalty and inspiring stories of sharing the gospel; to the Wynn family for their big hearts and great talent; and to Linda Moore for her bravery and enthusiasm.

And to the many people who have boldly spoken the Word of truth, including: Ellie C., Lottie, Linda, Philip D., Jay, Ellie J., Paul, Anna, Rachel S., Jim D., Ed B., Grace L., Brad C., Tim P., Jake, Jordan, Nathaniel, Anne, Rebecca G., Allison, Abigail, Hannah, Spencer, Casey, Nathaniel, Colin, Carly, Matty O., Dawn F., Ben, Wenyu, Mario, Katherine, Jeff N., Jeffrey N., Galen, Dan and Kyle, Mark and Bradley, Jen and Andrew, Deborah and Nicole, Carol G., Rebecca T., Tom A., Tom S., Robby, Connie, Gary S., Arturo, Nate, Edmund C., Tania S., Steve C., Mike L., Jay, Jae, Mark W-M., Mike V., Becky C., Philipp L., Käthe, Carsten, Peter S., Eaden, Benjamin E., Rebecca E., Kerry W., Titus L., Frank-Detlef, Lydia, Darren H., Lauren H., Rosana, Aleth, Thomas L., Gabby G., Liam W., Dan G., Igor, Charity, Aghiad, Esli, Felix, Sam C., Ryan, Steve G., Mishal,

Jeremy S., Mairi, Gary D., Eric H., Kelly K., Jim Cap., Natalie L., Kori, Imelda, Sujan, Sidney, Julian W., Jeanette, Jamari, Beth W., Michael, Natalie P., Lucille (there could only be one!), Regina, David F., Timothy K., Naomi W., Naomi B., Vishal, Nicolas, Verena, Iris, Stefan L., Charity, Raoul, Mike Mc., Abigail B., Kyla S., Ellie H., Sam P., Paige, Caleb (the youngest!), Chris G., Trevor, Bronwyn, ... and the one that I can't remember.

Appendix I
Technical Troubleshooting

In this technological world, there are bound to be times when we run up against some shortcomings in the setup. Even when your preparation has been flawless and your checklist is complete, technical problems can threaten to undermine all of the hard work that has been done.

Before you panic, breathe a bit and imagine the worst-case scenario. In this scenario, every piece of technology has decided to take the day off. There are no lights, no projector, and only a silent sound system. It is dark and quiet. People fidget in their seats as a few scurry about, trying to come to terms with whatever has caused the outage. Just imagine that.

Then imagine that your reciter stands up and raises his or her voice, speaking those beautiful words of healing, comfort, exhortation, and encouragement. Imagine it silent and still with just those words ringing through the air.

If that's the worst case, then we needn't worry. It sounds pretty good to me. Remember that when a technical glitch arises and somebody thinks it will ruin everything, it won't. You've already imagined the worst that it can be, and you know that it will be fine.

Methodology

If there is a problem, approach it in a methodical fashion. Although your first instinct might be to take a "shotgun approach," haphazardly wiggling connections, revising cabling, and modifying settings, a methodical approach will almost always find the problem with less effort and in a shorter amount of time.

The most basic troubleshooting technique (after "is it plugged in?") is to divide and conquer. This involves identifying the good parts of the system as well as figuring out which parts have failed. First, define what is working. Not only can these working sections be eliminated as the cause of the problem, but they can also be used to test other parts of the system. For example, imagine one mic channel at a mixer is dead while the others are operating properly. The good news is that you can use one of the working channels to isolate the problem.

Unplug an input connector from a working channel on the console and plug it into the dead channel. If it now works, the problem must exist before the console, back toward the mic. If it's still dead, the problem must be after that channel's input. With this one step, you have eliminated about half of the system as being the source of the problem.

Let's assume the console is okay. The remaining part of the system can be divided in half again by doing the same thing at the stage end of the snake. Switch the cables back to where they were on the console and plug a cable from a known working mic into the offending channel on the stage box. If the channel stays dead, the problem must be in the snake. But if the channel comes to life, the snake has been eliminated and the problem must be between the stage box and the mic (in the cable or even the mic itself). In this case, substituting either the mic cable or the actual mic will identify the problem.

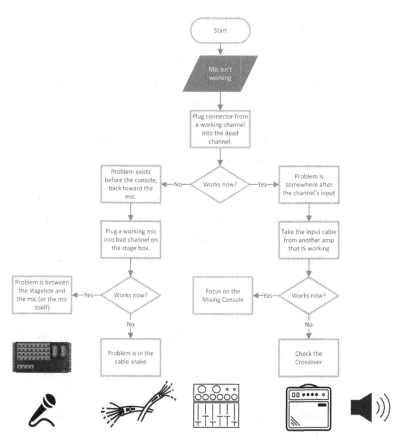

Divide and Conquer Sound System Troubleshooting

The tendency, especially under pressure, is to panic. Although you might just get lucky and hit on the defective component right away, it's easy to put yourself into an endless circle, trying this and that without really getting a handle on where the problem lies. This is especially true if a section has more than one defective component.

Practice an organized troubleshooting method, and you'll divide and conquer your problem every time.[17]

---

[17]   http://whirlwindusa.com/support/tech-articles/
basics-troubleshooting-sound-systems/.

Troubleshooting Sound Problems

- **Trouble**: Ear-piercing feedback.
  - o **Solution**: Stand behind the speakers. Move the mic as close as possible to the lips. Speak up. Turn the gain down.
  - o If these don't work, then there are feedback eliminators that can help reduce feedback (but not really eliminate it).

- **Trouble**: A low-level buzz or hum is heard in the speakers.
  - o **Solution One**: Turn off the mixer channels that are not needed during the recitation.
  - o **Solution Two**: Check for a bad microphone cable. Try replacing it.

- **Trouble**: Volume is too low.
  - o **Solution One**: Turn up the gain setting on the mixer.
  - o **Solution Two**: Some wireless mics have a gain setting in the bodypack that needs to be set for the specific mic plugged into it. If a mic is swapped from the bodypack with which it is normally used, the gain level can be way off.

- **Trouble**: A rustling or other unwanted sound is coming through the speakers.
  - o **Solution One**: Someone else's mic is on and it shouldn't be.
  - o **Solution Two**: Something is brushing against the microphone. Check for hair, fabric, jewelry, or body parts rubbing against the mic.
  - o **Solution Three:** The ventilation system is blowing onto the microphone.

Troubleshooting Lighting Problems

More light is not always the answer. Sometimes you may have enough light, but it is applied unevenly, and the extra hot light causes shadows.

- **Trouble:** Excessive shadows on the face, especially in eye sockets and under the nose.
  - o **Solution:** Either position the light mount lower or add a light from the front, pointing slightly upward.

- **Trouble:** Reciter leaves the boundary of the spotlight.
  - o **Solution:** A spotlight is another character onstage and so should be rehearsed. The reciter and spotlight operator need to work together. Unless the spotlight movements can be smooth, avoid moving the spot and instruct the reciter to stay within the boundaries of the light.

- **Trouble:** Reflecting surfaces cause distracting flashes of light.
  - o **Solution:** The source can be from behind the reciter, especially a guitar soundboard, or from the reciter's clothing or jewelry—or from some other shiny object. You can ask the reciter to avoid wearing reflective items, but the other surfaces may need to be noted and attended to during the sound check. Last-minute items are no fun, but this is one for which you want to keep a look out.

Troubleshooting Projection Problems

Projection problems run from the source itself, whether a document or a video, to the projector and screen. We are all so visually oriented that problems affecting our eyes distract us from the message.

- **Trouble**: Washed-out or dim image(s).
  - o **Solution**: Position of the projector, power of the projector lamp, age of the bulb (they die gradually), projector brightness setting.

- **Trouble**: Top of the image is wider or narrower than the bottom of the image (vertical trapezoid).
  - o **Solution**: Adjust the vertical keystone correction or raise or lower the projector. The problem is that the projector lens is not perpendicular to the screen.

- **Trouble**: One side of the image is wider or narrower than the other side (horizontal trapezoid).
  - o **Solution**: Adjust the horizontal keystone correction or move the projector toward the smaller side. The problem is that the projector lens is not perpendicular to the screen.

- **Trouble**: Noise from the projector is distracting.
  - o **Solution**: Move the projector up to a ceiling or high mount with a platform under it. You will also need to do a vertical keystone compensation. NOTE: *Do not put the projector in a box. That will lower the noise, but the heat generated will burn out bulbs faster and could damage the projector.*

Appendix II

Release Forms

Sample Release Forms

Grant

For consideration which I acknowledge, I grant to _____ ("Company") and Company's assigns, licensees, and successors, the right to use my image for all purposes, including advertising, trade, or any commercial purpose throughout the world and in perpetuity. I grant the right to use my name and image for the purposes listed above in all forms and media, including composite or modified representations, and waive the right to inspect or approve versions of my image used for publication or the written copy that may be used in connection with the images.

Release

I release Company and Company's assigns, licensees, and successors from any claims that may arise regarding the use of my image including any claims of defamation, invasion of privacy, or infringement of moral rights, rights of publicity, or copyright. Company is permitted, although not obligated, to include my name as a credit in connection with the image.

Name: _____

Date: _____

Signature: _____

Address: _____

Witness Signature: _____

Minors

In most jurisdictions, a minor is any person under eighteen years of age, but variations abound. It is best to check and not assume. Since a minor may not understand the terms of a release, the signature of a parent or guardian is required before using a minor's name or image.

Parent/Guardian Consent (if the person is under eighteen)

I am the parent or guardian of the minor named above. I have the legal right to consent to and do consent to the terms and conditions of this release.

Parent/Guardian Name: _____

Date: _____

Parent/Guardian Signature: _____

Parent/Guardian Address: _____

Witness Signature: _____

Print Release Form

Below is an example of the release form that I requested from anybody whose image appeared in the companion book to this one, entitled *The Art of Reciting Scripture.* I believe it provides both the publisher and me with enough protection and is a reasonable request of the person involved.

STANDARD RELEASE FORM

For use of photographs, audio files, video clips, biographical information, and quotations from interviews.

I, FirstName LastName (the "Licensor"), give my permission to include any images, video clips, audio files, biographical information, and interview quotations from which I may be identified (the "Material") in THE ART OF RECITING SCRIPTURE (the "Work") to be published by WestBow Press, a division of Thomas Nelson & Zondervan, or one of its affiliated companies ("WestBow"). I grant WestBow the right to use this Material:

- in the Work and in any related derivative and ancillary Works published by WestBow or its licensees
- for worldwide distribution
- in all formats and platforms in any and all media now known or hereafter developed
- in all editions, for the life of those editions without restriction
- in all languages
- in advertisements and promotional materials for the Work

I represent and warrant that (i) I am the sole owner of all copyright, trademark, and other intellectual property and proprietary rights in and to the Material, (ii) WestBow's publication of the Material as authorized herein will not violate or infringe any copyright, trademark, or other intellectual property or proprietary right of any person or entity, and (iii) I am not a party to and the Material is not subject to any contract or arrangement which would conflict with my permission herein.

This Agreement shall be governed by, and construed in

accordance with: 1) the laws of England and Wales, if the Licensor is located outside of the United States, or 2) the laws of the State of New York, if the Licensor is located in the United States. In relation to any legal action or proceedings to enforce this Agreement or arising out of or in connection with this Agreement each of the parties irrevocably submits to the exclusive jurisdiction of the courts: 1) in England and Wales, if the Licensor is located outside of the United States, or 2) in New York, New York, if the Licensor is located in the United States.

Please indicate your agreement by signing and returning this form. In signing, you warrant you have no claim on ground of breach of confidence or on any ground in any legal system against Thomas L. Griffin in respect of the publication of images of, or quotations from, you.

*If the subject is under the age of sixteen, consent should be given by a parent or guardian and the relationship to the subject indicated.

I/We hereby grant permission for the use of the material requested above.

Name of Subject / Parent / Guardian:

_____

FirstName_LastName

Signature of Subject / Parent / Guardian:

_____

Address:

_____

Street, City Postal Code, Country

Date:

_____

Appendix III

Lists

Top Ten Reasons to Recite

1. Because you have a bad memory (it's a muscle that should be exercised).
2. It's a biblical command (Deuteronomy 11:18–21).
3. It will help you to overcome your fear of public speaking.
4. You will be prepared to share the Word with others.
5. You will become a better communicator.
6. You will get to know more people in your church family.
7. Your church family will get to know you.
8. You will be a contributor.
9. You will be a witness to those around you.
10. It is the best Bible study ever; it will change how you study the Bible.

Common Mistakes to Identify in Rehearsal

1. Tailing off.
2. Wandering onstage.
3. Awkward hands.
4. Talking too fast.

Checklist for the Day of the Recitation

On the day of the recitation, ensure that you have completed the following:

- ✓ An order of worship and transitions have been defined, and all involved people have been notified.
- ✓ Arrangements have been made to move any onstage obstacles for the reciter.
- ✓ The person on-book has a copy of the text.
- ✓ A microphone has been positioned (especially the headset), and an onstage sound check has been completed.
- ✓ The reciter knows how to turn on and off the microphone.
- ✓ The reciter has arrived early and warmed up their voice.
- ✓ The reciter has performed a dry run of the passage.
- ✓ Graphics have been provided to the projection team.
- ✓ The projection team has been briefed on when graphics should be displayed.
- ✓ A video recorder is in place (optional).

Appendix IV

Multi-Voice Recitations

Multi-Voice Recitations - John 1:1-18 with two voices

RECITER	PASSAGE
Reciter #1	In the beginning was the Word, and the Word was with God, and the Word was God. He was in the beginning with God. All things were made through him, and without him was not any thing made that was made.
Reciter #2	In him was life, and the life was the light of men. The light shines in the darkness, and the darkness has not overcome it.
Reciter #1	There was a man sent from God, whose name was John. He came as a witness, to bear witness about the light, that all might believe through him. He was not the light, but came to bear witness about the light.
Reciter #2	The true light, which gives light to everyone, was coming into the world. He was in the world, and the world was made through him, yet the world did not know him. He came to his own, and his own people did not receive him. But to all who did receive him, who believed in his name, he gave the right to become children of God, who were born, not of blood nor of the will of the flesh nor of the will of man, but of God.

Reciter #1	And the Word became flesh and dwelt among us, and we have seen his glory, glory as of the only Son from the Father, full of grace and truth.
Reciter #2	(John bore witness about him, and cried out, "This was he of whom I said, 'He who comes after me ranks before me, because he was before me.'") For from his fullness we have all received, grace upon grace. For the law was given through Moses; grace and truth came through Jesus Christ.
Reciter #1	No one has ever seen God; the only God, who is at the Father's side, he has made him known.

Multi-Voice Recitations - Daniel 3:1-18 with three voices

RECITER	PASSAGE
Reciter #1	King Nebuchadnezzar made an image of gold, sixty cubits high and six cubits wide, and set it up on the plain of Dura in the province of Babylon.
Reciter #2	He then summoned the satraps,
Reciter #3	prefects,
Reciter #1	governors,
Reciter #1	advisers,
Reciter #2	treasurers,
Reciter #1	judges,
Reciter #2	magistrates
Reciter #3	and all the other provincial officials
Reciter #1	to come to the dedication of the image he had set up.
Reciter #2	So the satraps,
Reciter #3	prefects,
Reciter #1	governors,
Reciter #1	advisers,
Reciter #3	treasurers,
Reciter #1	judges,
Reciter #2	magistrates
Reciter #3	and all the other provincial officials
Reciter #2	assembled for the dedication of the image that King Nebuchadnezzar had set up, and they stood before it.
Reciter #1	Then the herald loudly proclaimed,
Reciter #2	"Nations and peoples of every language, this is what you are commanded to do: As soon as you hear the sound of the horn,
Reciter #1	flute,
Reciter #3	zither,
Reciter #2	lyre,
Reciter #1	harp,
Reciter #2	pipe

Reciter #3	and all kinds of music,
Reciter #2	all the nations and peoples of every language fell down
Reciter #1	and worshiped the image of gold that King Nebuchadnezzar had set up.
Reciter #3	At this time some astrologers came forward and denounced the Jews. They said to King Nebuchadnezzar,
Reciter #1	"May the king live forever!
Reciter #2	Your Majesty has issued a decree that everyone who hears the sound of the horn,
Reciter #1	flute,
Reciter #3	zither,
Reciter #2	lyre,
Reciter #1	harp,
Reciter #2	pipe
Reciter #3	and all kinds of music,
Reciter #2	must fall down and worship the image of gold, and that
Reciter #1	whoever does not fall down and worship will be thrown into a blazing furnace.
Reciter #3	But there are some Jews whom you have set over the affairs of the province of Babylon—
Reciter #2	Shadrach,
Reciter #3	Meshach
Reciter #1	and Abednego—
Reciter #3	who pay no attention to you, Your Majesty.
Reciter #2	They neither serve your gods nor worship the image of gold you have set up."
Reciter #1	Furious with rage, Nebuchadnezzar summoned
Reciter #2	Shadrach,
Reciter #3	Meshach
Reciter #1	and Abednego.
Reciter #2	So these men were brought before the king, and Nebuchadnezzar said to them,
Reciter #3	"Is it true,
Reciter #2	Shadrach,

Reciter #3	Meshach
Reciter #1	and Abednego.
Reciter #3	that you do not serve my gods or worship the image of gold I have set up?
Reciter #2	Now when you hear the sound of the horn,
Reciter #1	flute,
Reciter #3	zither,
Reciter #2	lyre,
Reciter #1	harp,
Reciter #2	pipe
Reciter #3	and all kinds of music,
Reciter #2	if you are ready to fall down and worship the image I made, very good.
Reciter #1	But if you do not worship it, you will be thrown immediately into a blazing furnace. Then what god will be able to rescue you from my hand?"
Reciter #2	Shadrach,
Reciter #3	Meshach
Reciter #1	and Abednego
Reciter #2	replied to him,
Reciter #3	"King Nebuchadnezzar, we do not need to defend ourselves before you in this matter.
Reciter #2	If we are thrown into the blazing furnace, the God we serve is able to deliver us from it, and he will deliver us from Your Majesty's hand.
Reciter #1	But even if he does not, we want you to know, Your Majesty,
Reciter #1, Reciter #2, Reciter #3	that we will not serve your gods or worship the image of gold you have set up."

Multi-Language Recitations

Multi-Language Recitations - Pentecost:
Acts 2:1-12 with five reciters

RECITER	PASSAGE
Reciter #1	When the day of Pentecost came, they were all together in one place. Suddenly a sound like the blowing of a violent wind came from heaven and filled the whole house where they were sitting. They saw what seemed to be tongues of fire that separated and came to rest on each of them. All of them were filled with the Holy Spirit and began to speak in other tongues as the Spirit enabled them.
	Reciters #2,3,4 & 5 come onstage and, at a low volume, repeatedly recite their passages all at once in their non-English languages. This is meant to provide a "low-hum" that does not drown out the voice of Reciter #1
Reciter #1	Now there were staying in Jerusalem God-fearing Jews from every nation under heaven. When they heard this sound, a crowd came together in bewilderment, because each one heard their own language being spoken. ⁷ Utterly amazed, they asked: "Aren't all these who are speaking Galileans? ⁸ Then how is it that each of us hears them in our native language? ⁹ Parthians, Medes and Elamites;
	The low-hum stops as Reciter #2 steps forward
Reciter #2	Béni soit l'Éternel! Car il a signalé sa grâce envers moi, Comme si j'avais été dans une ville forte. (Psalm 31:21 LSG)
Reciter #1	residents of Mesopotamia, Judea and Cappadocia, Pontus and Asia,

Reciter #3	你奇妙的作为使远在地极的人心生敬畏，你使日出之地和日落之处都传来欢呼声(Psalm 65:8 CCB)
Reciter #1	Phrygia and Pamphylia, Egypt and the parts of Libya near Cyrene; visitors from Rome (both Jews and converts to Judaism);
Reciter #4	Die Himmel erzählen die Herrlichkeit Gottes, und die Ausdehnung verkündigt das Werk seiner Hände. (Psalm 19:1 SCH2000)
Reciter #1	Cretans and Arabs
Reciter #5	दिन के समय में तेरे लिये सूर्य का प्रकाश नहीं होगा और रात के समय में चाँद का प्रकाश तेरी रोशनी नहीं होगी। क्यों क्योंकि यहोवा ही सदैव तेरे लिये प्रकाश होगा। तेरा परमेश्वर तेरी महिमा बनेगा। (Isaiah 60:19 ERV-HI)
Reciter #2	Praise be to the Lord, for he showed me the wonders of his love when I was in a city under siege.. (Psalm 31:21)
Reciter #3	The whole earth is filled with awe at your wonders; where morning dawns, where evening fades, you call forth songs of joy.. (Psalm 65:8)
Reciter #4	The heavens declare the glory of God; the skies proclaim the work of his hands.. (Psalm 19:1)
Reciter #5	The sun will no more be your light by day, nor will the brightness of the moon shine on you, for the Lord will be your everlasting light, and your God will be your glory.. (Isaiah 60:19)
Reciter #1	Amazed and perplexed, they asked one another, "What does this mean?"

Multi-Language Recitations - 1 Corinthians 9:19-23 in two languages

RECITER	PASSAGE
Reciter #1	Ich bin also frei und keinem Menschen gegenüber zu irgendetwas verpflichtet.
Reciter #2	*Though I am free and belong to no one,*
Reciter #1	Und doch habe ich mich zum Sklaven aller gemacht, um möglichst viele 'für Christus' zu gewinnen.
Reciter #2	*I have made myself a slave to everyone, to win as many as possible.*
Reciter #1	Wenn ich mit Juden zu tun habe, verhalte ich mich wie ein Jude, um die Juden zu gewinnen.
Reciter #2	*To the Jews I became like a Jew, to win the Jews.*
Reciter #1	Wenn ich mit denen zu tun habe, die dem Gesetz des Moses unterstehen, verhalte ich mich so, als wäre ich ebenfalls dem Gesetz des Mose unterstellt (obwohl das nicht mehr der Fall ist); denn ich möchte auch diese Menschen gewinnen.
Reciter #2	*To those under the law I became like one under the law (though I myself am not under the law), so as to win those under the law.*
Reciter #1	Wenn ich mit denen zu tun habe, die das Gesetz des Moses nicht kennen, verhalte ich mich so, als würde ich es ebenfalls nicht kennen; denn auch sie möchte ich gewinnen. (Das bedeutet allerdings nicht, dass mein Leben mit Gott nicht doch einem Gesetz untersteht; ich bin ja an das Gesetz gebunden, das Christus uns gegeben hat.)
Reciter #2	*To those not having the law I became like one not having the law (though I am not free from God's law but am under Christ's law), so as to win those not having the law*

Reciter #1	Und wenn ich mit Menschen zu tun habe, deren Gewissen empfindlich ist, verzichte ich auf meine Freiheit, weil ich auch diese Menschen gewinnen möchte.
Reciter #2	*To the weak I became weak, to win the weak.*
Reciter #1	In jedem einzelnen Fall nehme ich jede nur erdenkliche Rücksicht auf die, mit denen ich es gerade zu tun habe, um jedes Mal wenigstens einige zu retten.
Reciter #2	*I have become all things to all people so that by all possible means I might save some.*
Reciter #1	Das alles tue ich wegen des Evangeliums;
Reciter #2	*I do all this for the sake of the gospel,*
Reciter #1	denn ich möchte an dem Segen teilhaben, den diese Botschaft bringt.
Reciter #2	*that I may share in its blessings.*

Point-Counterpoint
Recitations

Point-Counterpoint Recitations - The Juxtaposition of Psalm 18:30-33 & Romans 3:10-17

RECITER	PASSAGE
Reciter #1	Wie steht es also? Haben wir (Juden) für uns etwas voraus? Nicht unbedingt. Wir haben ja schon vorhin gegen Juden ebenso wie gegen Griechen die Anklage erheben müssen, dass sie ausnahmslos unter (der Herrschaft) der Sünde stehen, wie es in der Schrift heißt: „Es gibt keinen Gerechten, auch nicht einen; es gibt keinen Einsichtigen, keinen, der Gott mit Ernst sucht; sie sind alle abgewichen, allesamt entartet; keiner ist da, der das Gute tut, auch nicht ein Einziger." „Ein offenes Grab ist ihre Kehle, mit ihren Zungen reden sie Trug." „Otterngift ist unter ihren Lippen." „Ihr Mund ist voll Fluchens und Bitterkeit." „Schnell sind ihre Füße, Blut zu vergießen; Verwüstung und Unheil sind auf ihren Wegen und den Weg des Friedens kennen sie nicht.
Reciter #1	As it is written: "There is no one righteous, not even one; there is no one who understands
Reciter #2	As for God, his way is perfect; The Lord's word is flawless
Reciter #1	there is no one who seeks God
Reciter #2	he shields all who take refuge in him.
Reciter #1	All have turned away, they have together become worthless; there is no one who does good, not even one"
Reciter #2	For who is God besides the Lord? And who is the Rock except our God?
Reciter #1	Their throats are open graves; their tongues practice deceit." „The poison of vipers is on their lips."

Reciter #2	It is God who arms me with strength and keeps my way secure.
Reciter #1	„Their mouths are full of cursing and bitterness." „Their feet are swift to shed blood;
Reciter #2	Her makes my feet like the feet of a deer; he causes me to stand on the heights.
Reciter #1	ruin and misery mark their ways, and the way of peace they do not know.
Reciter #2	As for God, his way is perfect; The Lord's word is flawless; he shields all who take refuge in him. For who is God besides the Lord? And who is the Rock except our God? It is God who arms me with strength and keeps my way secure. Her makes my feet like the feet of a deer; he causes me to stand on the heights.

Group Recitations

Group Recitations - Father's Day Advice from Kids

RECITER	PASSAGE
Worship Leader	We've heard advice from experienced dads, and it was really good. But I wonder if kids have advice for fathers. Are there any kids who have some advice for dads?
	kids run up and surround the worship leader
Worship Leader	So you have some advice, do you? Of course, we want to make sure that your advice is sound, so I expect that you have a verse from the Bible that will back up your advice
	kids become quiet, contemplating what was said, and sit down on the stage steps, assuming the "Thinker" pose
Worship Leader	Gary: Do you have a great dad?
Reciter #1	Yes, I do.
Worship Leader	Do you love your dad?
Reciter #1	Yes, I do.
Worship Leader	Do you have some advice?
Reciter #1	Yes, I do.
Worship Leader	What is your advice?
Reciter #1	First of all, love the Lord. Proverbs 14:26 In the fear of the Lord one has strong confidence, and his children will have a refuge.
	Reciter#1 steps down (maybe high-five from the worship leader) Reciter #2 steps up

Worship Leader	Hello, Reciter #2, what is your advice?
Reciter #2	Be kind. Psalm 103:13 As a father shows compassion to his children, so the LORD shows compassion to those who fear him.
	Reciter#2 steps down (maybe high-five from the worship leader) *Reciter #3 steps up*
Worship Leader	Hello, Reciter #3, what is your advice?
Reciter #3	Be thoughtful. Ephesians 6:4 Fathers, do not provoke your children to anger, but bring them up in the discipline and instruction of the Lord.
	Reciter#3 steps down (maybe high-five from the worship leader) *Reciter #4 steps up*
Worship Leader	Hello, Reciter #4, what is your advice?
Reciter #4	Be honest. Proverbs 20:7 The righteous who walks in his integrity—blessed are his children after him!
	Reciter#4 steps down (maybe high-five from the worship leader) *Reciter #5 steps up*
Worship Leader	Hello, Reciter #5, what is your advice?
Reciter #5	Be wise with your money. Proverbs 13:22 A good man leaves an inheritance to his children's children, but the sinner's wealth is laid up for the righteous.

	Reciter#5 steps down (maybe high-five from the worship leader) *Reciter #6 steps up*
Worship Leader	Hello, Reciter #6, what do you want to share with fathers?
Reciter #6	But while he was still a long way off, his father saw him and was filled with compassion for him; he ran to his son, threw his arms around him and kissed him. Matthew 15:20b

Group Recitations - Father's Day Advice from Dads

RECITER	PASSAGE
Reciter #1	Husbands, love your wives, just as Christ loved the church and gave himself up for her to make her holy, cleansing her by the washing with water through the word, and to present her to himself as a radiant church, without stain or wrinkle or any other blemish, but holy and blameless. In this same way, husbands ought to love their wives as their own bodies. He who loves his wife loves himself. Ephesians 5:25-28 (NIV)
Reciter #2	These commandments that I give you today are to be on your hearts. Impress them on your children. Talk about them when you sit at home and when you walk along the road, when you lie down and when you get up. Tie them as symbols on your hands and bind them on your foreheads. Write them on the doorframes of your houses and on your gates. Deuteronomy 6:6-9 (NIV)
Reciter #3	Start children off on the way they should go, and even when they are old they will not turn from it. Proverbs 22:6 (NIV)
Reciter #4	Whoever fears the Lord has a secure fortress, and for their children it will be a refuge. Proverbs 14:26 (NIV)
Reciter #5	As a father has compassion on his children, so the Lord has compassion on those who fear him; Psalm 103:13 (NIV)
Reciter #6	But if serving the Lord seems undesirable to you, then choose for yourselves this day whom you will serve, whether the gods your ancestors served beyond the Euphrates, or the gods of the Amorites, in whose land you are living. But as for me and my household, we will serve the Lord." Joshua 24:15 (NIV)

Group Recitations - Psalm 51 in Nine Languages

RECITER	SPOKEN TEXT	ENGLISH TRANSLATION
All Language Reciters together in English	Have mercy on me, O God, according to your unfailing love	Have mercy on me, O God, according to your unfailing love
Tamil	தேவனே, உமத கிருபையின்படி எனக்கு இரங்கும்,	Have mercy on me, O God, according to your unfailing love
Croatian	Smiluj mi se, Bože, po milosrđu svome, po velikom smilovanju	Have mercy on me, O God, according to your unfailing love
French	Toi dont le cœur est si grand, Efface mes désobéissances	according to your great compassion blot out my transgressions
Spanish	Lávame más y más de mi maldad	and cleanse me from my sin
French	et purifie-moi de ma faute.	and cleanse me from my sin
Tamil	என் பாவமற என்னைச் சுத்திகரியும்.	and cleanse me from my sin
German	und reinige mich von meiner Sünde	and cleanse me from my sin
Chinese (Cantonese)	潔除我的罪！	and cleanse me from my sin
Arabic (Syrian)	وَمِنْ خَطِيَّتِي طَهِّرْنِي.	and cleanse me from my sin
Croatian	od grijeha me mojeg očisti!	and cleanse me from my sin

Swahili	Unitakase dhambi zangu	and cleanse me from my sin
Spanish	Y límpiame de mi pecado.	and cleanse me from my sin
Arabic (Syrian)	لأَنِّي عَارِفٌ بِمَعَاصِيَّ، وَخَطِيَّتِي أَمَامِي دَائِمًا.	For I know my transgressions, and my sin is always before me.
English	Against you, you only, have I sinned and done what is evil in your sight;	Against you, you only, have I sinned and done what is evil in your sight;
German	Du bist im Recht mit deinem Urteil	so you are right in your verdict
Chinese (Cantonese)	判斷的時候顯為清白	and justified when you judge.
Swahili	Tazama, nikazaliwa nikiwa na hatia. Mama yangu akanichukua mimba nikiwa na dhambi	Surely I was sinful at birth, sinful from the time my mother conceived me
Spanish	He aquí, tú amas la verdad en lo íntimo, Y en lo secreto me has hecho comprender sabiduría.	yet you desired faithfulness even in the womb; you taught me wisdom in that secret place.
Tamil	நீர் என்னை ஈசோப்பினால் சுத்திகரியும், அப்பொழுது நான் சுத்தமாவேன்; என்னைக் கழுவியரளும், அப்பொழுது நான் உறைந்த மழையிலும் வெண்மையாவேன்.	Cleanse me with hyssop, and I will be clean; wash me, and I will be whiter than snow.

127

Swahili	Unifanye kusikia furaha na shangwe, Mifupa uliyoiponda ifurahi.	Let me hear joy and gladness; let the bones you have crushed rejoice.
Croatian	Objavi mi radost i veselje, nek' se obraduju kosti satrvene!	Let me hear joy and gladness; let the bones you have crushed rejoice.
French	Détourné ton regard de mes fautes,Efface tous mes torts.	Hide your face from my sins and blot out all my iniquity.
English	Create in me a pure heart, O God,	Create in me a pure heart, O God,
Arabic (Syrian)	Create in me a pure heart, O God, *(begin after previous reciter says "…heart")*	Create in me a pure heart, O God,
Croatian	Create in me a pure heart, O God, *(begin after previous reciter says "…heart")*	Create in me a pure heart, O God,
Tamil	Create in me a pure heart, O God, *(begin after previous reciter says "…heart")*	Create in me a pure heart, O God,
German	Create in me a pure heart, O God, *(begin after previous reciter says "…heart")*	Create in me a pure heart, O God,
French	Create in me a pure heart, O God, *(begin after previous reciter says "…heart")*	Create in me a pure heart, O God,
Chinese (Cantonese)	Create in me a pure heart, O God, *(begin after previous reciter says "…heart")*	Create in me a pure heart, O God,
Spanish	Create in me a pure heart, O God, *(begin after previous reciter says "…heart")*	Create in me a pure heart, O God,

Swahili	Create in me a pure heart, O God, *(begin after previous reciter says "...heart")*	Create in me a pure heart, O God,
All Languages	And renew a steadfast spirit within me	And renew a steadfast spirit within me
German	Schick mich nicht weg aus deiner Nähe und nimm deinen Heiligen Geist nicht von mir!	Do not cast me from your presence, or take your Holy Spirit from me
Spanish	Vuélveme el gozo de tu salvación,	Restore to me the joy of your salvation
Reciter	Spoken Text	English translation
Arabic (Syrian)	وَبِرُوحٍ مُنْتَدِبَةٍ اعْضُدْنِ	And grant me a willing spirit to sustain me.
Croatian	i učvrsti me duhom spremnim!	And grant me a willing spirit to sustain me.
Tamil	உற்சாகமான ஆவி என்னைத் தாங்கூம்படி செய்யும்.	And grant me a willing spirit to sustain me.
German	Hilf mir, indem du mich bereit machst, dir gerne zu gehorchen.	And grant me a willing spirit to sustain me.
French	Renouvelle et affermis mon esprit.	And grant me a willing spirit to sustain me.
Chinese (Cantonese)	賜我樂意的靈扶持我	And grant me a willing spirit to sustain me.
Spanish	Y espíritu noble me sustente.	And grant me a willing spirit to sustain me.

Swahili	Unitegemeze kwa roho ya upendo.	And grant me a willing spirit to sustain me.
English	And grant me a willing spirit to sustain me.	And grant me a willing spirit to sustain me.
English	Please join us in reciting Psalm 51	Please join us in reciting Psalm 51

Group Recitations - True Religion

RECITER	ENGLISH TEXT
Reciter #1	"To the Lord your God belong the heavens, even the highest heavens, the earth and everything in it.
Reciter #2	The multitude of your sacrifices— what are they to me?" says the Lord. "I have more than enough of burnt offerings, of rams and the fat of fattened animals; I have no pleasure in the blood of bulls and lambs and goats. When you come to appear before me, who has asked this of you, this trampling of my courts?" Stop bringing meaningless offerings!
Reciter #3	If anyone considers himself religious and yet does not keep a tight rein on his tongue, he deceives himself and his religion is worthless.
Reciter #1	Yet the Lord set his affection on your forefathers and loved them, and he chose you, their descendants, above all the nations, as it is today. Circumcise your hearts, therefore, and do not be stiff-necked any longer.
Reciter #2	Your hands are full of blood; wash and make yourselves clean. Take your evil deeds out of my sight!
Reciter #1	For the Lord your God is God of gods and Lord of lords, the great God, mighty and awesome, who shows no partiality and accepts no bribes.
Reciter #2	Stop doing wrong, learn to do right! Seek justice, encourage the oppressed.
Reciter #1	He defends the cause of the fatherless and the widow, and loves the alien, giving him food and clothing.
Reciter #1	This is what the Lord Almighty says: "Give careful thought to your ways.
Reciter #3	Religion that God our Father accepts as pure and faultless is this: to look after orphans and widows in their distress and to keep oneself from being polluted by the world.
Reciter #2	And you are to love those who are aliens, for you yourselves were aliens in Egypt.

Group Recitations - The Quilt with Interviews

RECITER	PASSAGE
	The panel of speakers all sit for the transition by teaching pastor. After the introducion, the teaching pastor calls them up one at a time. Following is an example of how the flow would occur.
Teaching Pastor	*Transition comments by the teaching pastor.*
Reciter #1	Today I have given you the choice between life and death, between blessings and curses. Now I call on heaven and earth to witness the choice you make. Oh, that you would choose life, so that you and your descendants might live! You can make this choice by loving the Lord your God, obeying him, and committing yourself firmly to him. This is the key to your life Deut 30:19-20a
Reciter #2	Don't copy the behavior and customs of this world, but let God transform you into a new person by changing the way you think. Then you will learn to know God's will for you, which is good and pleasing and perfect. Romans 12:2 (NLT)
Teaching Pastor	*<Asks something about the passage or about its significance to the reciters>*
Reciter #1 & #2	*<describes the significance of the passage or something that was learned in the process of memorizing it>*
	Transition as Reciters #1 and #2 sit down and reciters #3 and #4 rise.
Reciter #3	Have I not commanded you? Be strong and of good courage; do not be afraid, nor be dismayed, for the Lord your God is with you wherever you go. Joshua 1:9 NKJV
Reciter #4	For God did not give us a spirit of timidity but one of power, love, and self-discipline. 2 Timothy 1:7

Teaching Pastor	*\<Asks something about the passage or about its significance to the reciter\>*
Reciters #3 & #4	*\<describes the significance of the passage or something that was learned in the process of memorizing it\>*
Reciter #5	Don't let anyone look down on you because you are young, but set an example for the believers in speech, in conduct, in love, in faith and in purity. 1 Timothy 4:12
Teaching Pastor	*\<Asks something about the passage or about its significance to the reciter\>*
Reciters #5	*\<describes the significance of the passage or something that was learned in the process of memorizing it\>*
Reciter #1	Oh people, the Lord has told you what is good, and this is what he requires of you; to do what is right, to love mercy and to walk humbly with your God. Micah 6:8 NLT
Teaching Pastor	*\<Asks something about the passage or about its significance to the reciter\>*
Reciter #1	*\<describes the significance of the passage or something that was learned in the process of memorizing it\>*
Reciter #2	Don't just pretend to love others. Really love them. Hate what is wrong. Hold tightly to what is good. Love each other with genuine affection, and take delight in honoring each other. Romans 12:9-10
Reciter #3	But love your enemies, do good, and lend, hoping for nothing in return; and your reward will be great, and you will be sons of the Most High. For He is kind to the unthankful and evil. Luke 6:35 NKJV
Reciter #4	In the same way, let your light shine before others, that they may see your good deeds and glorify your Father in heaven. Matt 5:16

Teaching Pastor	*<Asks something about the passage or about its significance to the reciter>*
Reciters #2, 3 & 4	*<describes the significance of the passage or something that was learned in the process of memorizing it>*
	The final recitation may be done as a benediction
Reciter #5	In all my prayers for all of you, I always pray with joy because of your partnership in the gospel from the first day until now, being confident of this, that he who began a good work in you will carry it on to completion until the day of Christ Jesus. Philippians 1:4-6

Audience Participation Recitations

Audience Participation Recitations – The Attributes of God

ATTRIBUTE	PERSON	PASSAGE
	Worship Leader	You see the list of Attributes of God. The challenge for you is to listen to the passage that is about to be recited and then decide which attribute the passage describes.
Immense	Reciter	"But will God really dwell on earth? The heavens, even the highest heaven, cannot contain you. How much less this temple I have built! This is what the Lord says: "Heaven is my throne, and the earth is my footstool. Where is the house you will build for me? Where will my resting place be? Kings 8:27
Immense	Reciter	This is what the Lord says: "Heaven is my throne, and the earth is my footstool. Where is the house you will build for me? Where will my resting place be? Isaiah 66:1
Infinite	Reciter	Your love, Lord, reaches to the heavens, your faithfulness to the skies. Your righteousness is like the highest mountains, your justice like the great deep. You, Lord, preserve both people and animals. Psalm 36:5-6

Infinite	Reciter	How great is God—beyond our understanding! The number of his years is past finding out. Job 36:26
Good	Reciter	"Which of you, if your son asks for bread, will give him a stone? Or if he asks for a fish, will give him a snake? If you, then, though you are evil, know how to give good gifts to your children, how much more will your Father in heaven give good gifts to those who ask him! Matthew 7:9-11 (same as Luke 11:11)
Perfect	Reciter	The law of the Lord is perfect, refreshing the soul. The statutes of the Lord are trustworthy, making wise the simple. The precepts of the Lord are right, giving joy to the heart. The commands of the Lord are radiant, giving light to the eyes. The fear of the Lord is pure, enduring forever. The decrees of the Lord are firm, and all of them are righteous.They are more precious than gold, than much pure gold; they are sweeter than honey, than honey from the honeycomb. By them your servant is warned; in keeping them there is great reward. Psalm 19:7-11
Just	Reciter	The Lord reigns forever; he has established his throne for judgment. He rules the world in righteousness and judges the peoples with equity. Psalm 9:7-8

Omnipresent	Reciter	Where can I go from your Spirit? Where can I flee from your presence? If I go up to the heavens, you are there; if I make my bed in the depths, you are there. If I rise on the wings of the dawn, if I settle on the far side of the sea, even there your hand will guide me, your right hand will hold me fast. If I say, "Surely the darkness will hide me and the light become night around me," even the darkness will not be dark to you; the night will shine like the day, for darkness is as light to you. Psalm 139:7-12
Immanent	Reciter	Therefore the Lord himself will give you a sign: The virgin will conceive and give birth to a son, and will call him Immanuel. Isaiah 7:14
Graceful	Reciter	But God demonstrates his own love for us in this: While we were still sinners, Christ died for us. Romans 5:8

Merciful	Reciter	The Lord is compassionate and gracious, slow to anger, abounding in love. He will not always accuse, nor will he harbor his anger forever; he does not treat us as our sins deserve or repay us according to our iniquities. For as high as the heavens are above the earth, so great is his love for those who fear him; as far as the east is from the west, so far has he removed our transgressions from us. As a father has compassion on his children, so the Lord has compassion on those who fear him; for he knows how we are formed, he remembers that we are dust. The life of mortals is like grass, they flourish like a flower of the field; the wind blows over it and it is gone, and its place remembers it no more. But from everlasting to everlasting the Lord's love is with those who fear him, and his righteousness with their children's children—with those who keep his covenant and remember to obey his precepts. Psalm 103:8-18
Merciful	Reciter	The Lord is not slow in keeping his promise, as some understand slowness. Instead he is patient with you, not wanting anyone to perish, but everyone to come to repentance. 2Peter 3:9

Merciful	Reciter	Say to them, 'As surely as I live, declares the Sovereign Lord, I take no pleasure in the death of the wicked, but rather that they turn from their ways and live. Turn! Turn from your evil ways! Why will you die, people of Israel?' Ezekiel 33:11
Holy	Reciter	At the sound of their voices the doorposts and thresholds shook and the temple was filled with smoke. "Woe to me!" I cried. "I am ruined! For I am a man of unclean lips, and I live among a people of unclean lips, and my eyes have seen the King, the Lord Almighty." Isaiah 6:4-5

Holy Day Recitations

Holy Day Recitations - Christmas Eve Prophecy

RECITER	PASSAGE
Worship Leader	The chosen one would be the Seed of Eve
Reciter #1	Then the Lord God said to the woman, "What is this that you have done?" The woman said, "The serpent deceived me, and I ate." The Lord God said to the serpent, "Because you have done this, cursed are you above all livestock and above all beasts of the field; on your belly you shall go, and dust you shall eat all the days of your life. I will put enmity between you and the woman, and between your offspring and her offspring; he shall bruise your head, and you shall bruise his heel." Genesis 3:13-15 (ESV)
Worship Leader	Born to a family shaped by prophecy. He would be in the line of Noah's son, Shem.
Reciter #2	"Blessed be the Lord, the God of Shem; and let Canaan be his servant. May God enlarge Japheth, and let him dwell in the tents of Shem, and let Canaan be his servant." Genesis 12:1-3 (ESV)
Worship Leader	A descendant of Abraham...
Reciter #3	Now the Lord said to Abram, "Go from your country and your kindred and your father's house to the land that I will show you. And I will make of you a great nation, and I will bless you and make your name great, so that you will be a blessing. I will bless those who bless you, and him who dishonors you I will curse, and in you all the families of the earth shall be blessed." Genesis 12:1-3 (ESV)

Worship Leader	A descendant of Isaac…
Reciter #2	Stay in this land for a while, and I will be with you and will bless you. For to you and your descendants I will give all these lands and will confirm the oath I swore to your father Abraham. I will make your descendants as numerous as the stars in the sky and will give them all these lands, and through your offspring all nations on earth will be blessed, Genesis 26:3-4 (NIV)
Worship Leader	And a descendant of Jacob.
Reciter #3	And God said to him (Jacob), "I am God Almighty; be fruitful and increase in number. A nation and a community of nations will come from you, and kings will be among your descendants. The land I gave to Abraham and Isaac I also give to you, and I will give this land to your descendants after you." Genesis 35:11-12 (NIV)
Worship Leader	He would come from the tribe of Judah…
Reciter #2	The scepter shall not depart from Judah, nor the ruler's staff from between his feet, until tribute comes to him; and to him shall be the obedience of the peoples. Genesis 49:10 (NIV)
Worship Leader	…and from the family line of Jesse
Reciter #3	A shoot will come up from the stump of Jesse; from his roots a Branch will bear fruit. Isaiah 11:1 (NIV)

Worship Leader	An offspring of the house of David.
Reciter #2	"Now then, tell my servant David, 'This is what the Lord Almighty says: I took you from the pasture, from tending the flock, and appointed you ruler over my people Israel. I have been with you wherever you have gone, and I have cut off all your enemies from before you. Now I will make your name great, like the names of the greatest men on earth. And I will provide a place for my people Israel and will plant them so that they can have a home of their own and no longer be disturbed. Wicked people will not oppress them anymore, as they did at the beginning and have done ever since the time I appointed leaders over my people Israel. I will also give you rest from all your enemies. "'The Lord declares to you that the Lord himself will establish a house for you: When your days are over and you rest with your ancestors, I will raise up your offspring to succeed you, your own flesh and blood, and I will establish his kingdom. 2 Samuel 7:8-12 (NIV)
Worship Leader	In a place foretold
Reciter #4	But you, O Bethlehem Ephrathah, who are too little to be among the clans of Judah, from you shall come forth for me one who is to be ruler in Israel, whose coming forth is from of old, from ancient days. Micah 5:2 (ESV)

Worship Leader	For a purpose that God pre-ordained
Reciter #1	He was oppressed and afflicted, yet he did not open his mouth; he was led like a lamb to the slaughter, and as a sheep before its shearers is silent, so he did not open his mouth. By oppression and judgment he was taken away. Yet who of his generation protested? For he was cut off from the land of the living; for the transgression of my people he was punished. He was assigned a grave with the wicked, and with the rich in his death, though he had done no violence, nor was any deceit in his mouth. Yet it was the Lord's will to crush him and cause him to suffer, and though the Lord makes his life an offering for sin, he will see his offspring and prolong his days, and the will of the Lord will prosper in his hand. After he has suffered, he will see the light of life and be satisfied; by his knowledge my righteous servant will justify many, and he will bear their iniquities. Therefore I will give him a portion among the great, and he will divide the spoils with the strong, because he poured out his life unto death, and was numbered with the transgressors. For he bore the sin of many, and made intercession for the transgressors. Isaiah 53:7-12 (NIV)
Worship Leader	So that we could know him
Reciter #5	Who has believed our message and to whom has the arm of the Lord been revealed? He grew up before him like a tender shoot, and like a root out of dry ground. He had no beauty or majesty to attract us to him, nothing in his appearance that we should desire him. He was despised and rejected by mankind, a man of suffering, and familiar with pain. Like one from whom people hide their faces he was despised, and we held him in low esteem. Isaiah 53:1-3 (NIV)

Worship Leader	So that we could know him
Reciter #4	"And I will pour out on the house of David and the inhabitants of Jerusalem a spirit of grace and supplication Zechariah 12:10a (NIV)
Worship Leader	At the right time
Reciter #5	But when the fullness of time had come, God sent forth his Son, born of woman, born under the law, to redeem those who were under the law, so that we might receive adoption as sons. Galatians 4:4-5 (ESV)
Worship Leader	To a woman foretold by Isaiah
Reciter #1	as he considered these things, behold, an angel of the Lord appeared to him in a dream, saying, "Joseph, son of David, do not fear to take Mary as your wife, for that which is conceived in her is from the Holy Spirit. She will bear a son, and you shall call his name Jesus, for he will save his people from their sins." All this took place to fulfill what the Lord had spoken by the prophet: "Behold, the virgin shall conceive and bear a son, and they shall call his name Immanuel" (which means, God with us). Matthew 1:20-23 (ESV)

Worship Leader	To a family shaped by prophecy
Reciter #6	In those days Caesar Augustus issued a decree that a census should be taken of the entire Roman world. (This was the first census that took place while Quirinius was governor of Syria.) And everyone went to their own town to register. So Joseph also went up from the town of Nazareth in Galilee to Judea, to Bethlehem the town of David, because he belonged to the house and line of David. He went there to register with Mary, who was pledged to be married to him and was expecting a child. While they were there, the time came for the baby to be born, and she gave birth to her firstborn, a son. She wrapped him in cloths and placed him in a manger, because there was no guest room available for them. <div align="right">Luke 2:1-7 (NIV)</div>
Worship Leader	In a place foretold by Micah
Reciter #4	After Jesus was born in Bethlehem in Judea, during the time of King Herod, Magi from the east came to Jerusalem and asked, "Where is the one who has been born king of the Jews? We saw his star when it rose and have come to worship him." When King Herod heard this he was disturbed, and all Jerusalem with him. When he had called together all the people's chief priests and teachers of the law, he asked them where the Messiah was to be born. "In Bethlehem in Judea," they replied, "for this is what the prophet has written: "'But you, Bethlehem, in the land of Judah, are by no means least among the rulers of Judah; for out of you will come a ruler who will shepherd my people Israel.'" <div align="right">Matthew 2:1-6 (NIV)</div>

Worship Leader	For a purpose that God pre-ordained

Reciter #2	even as he chose us in him before the foundation of the world, that we should be holy and blameless before him. In love he predestined us for adoption to himself as sons through Jesus Christ, according to the purpose of his will,
	                                                Ephesians 1:4-5 (ESV)
	far above all rule and authority and power and dominion, and above every name that is named, not only in this age but also in the one to come. And he put all things under his feet and gave him as head over all things to the church, which is his body, the fullness of him who fills all in all.
	                                                Ephesians 1: 21-23 (ESV)

Worship Leader	So that we can know Him
Reciter #5	"Therefore, my friends, I want you to know that through Jesus the forgiveness of sins is proclaimed to you. Through him everyone who believes is set free from every sin, a justification you were not able to obtain under the law of Moses. Acts 13:38-39 (NIV)
Worship Leader	So that we can know Him
Reciter #3	He committed no sin, neither was deceit found in his mouth. When he was reviled, he did not revile in return; when he suffered, he did not threaten, but continued entrusting himself to him who judges justly. He himself bore our sins in his body on the tree, that we might die to sin and live to righteousness. By his wounds you have been healed. 1Peter 2:22-24 (NIV)

Worship Leader	So that we can know Him
Reciter #1	and from Jesus Christ, who is the faithful witness, the firstborn from the dead, and the ruler of the kings of the earth. To him who loves us and has freed us from our sins by his blood, Revelation 1:5b (NIV)

About the Author

A software consultant with over a decade of teaching high school physics in his past, Tom grew up in San Leandro, California, where he found the love of his life, Carol. He started reciting Scripture in 1997 and has led hundreds of people through the process of preparing to recite. He has worked with individuals, small teams and large groups, developing the craft of recitations extending from single passages to complex multi-lingual compositions. Blessed with two incredible daughters and the best friends one could imagine, Tom now lives in Frankfurt, Germany where he practices as a consultant and coordinates recitations at the International Christian Fellowship.

Printed in the United States
by Baker & Taylor Publisher Services